React.js Essentials

A fast-paced guide to designing and building scalable and maintainable web apps with React.js

Artemij Fedosejev

PUBLISHING

BIRMINGHAM - MUMBAI

React.js Essentials

Copyright © 2015 Packt Publishing

First published: August 2015

Production reference: 1250815

Published by Packt Publishing Ltd.
Livery Place
35 Livery Street
Birmingham B3 2PB, UK.

ISBN 978-1-78355-162-0

www.packtpub.com

Credits

Author
Artemij Fedosejev

Reviewers
Denis Radin

Sander Spies

Konstantin Tarkus

Commissioning Editor
Dipika Gaonkar

Acquisition Editor
Nikhil Karkal

Content Development Editor
Pooja Nair

Technical Editor
Pramod Kumavat

Copy Editor
Rashmi Sawant

Project Coordinator
Bijal Patel

Proofreader
Safis Editing

Indexer
Priya Sane

Graphics
Sheetal Aute

Production Coordinator
Shantanu N. Zagade

Cover Work
Shantanu N. Zagade

Foreword

Are you tired of writing jQuery callback soup? Does your blood boil when you need to write yet another template or configuration in your Angular app? Wondering why your application structure is so complex? If so, React.js is what you've been looking for. The declarative nature of React.js will help you build a UI for large applications with data that changes over time.

As a professional iOS and JavaScript frontend consultant, I always recommend that clients use the best technology available. With the latest push from Facebook, React.js has proven itself to be a solid choice to build maintainable and performant user interfaces that help our clients ship products and move fast. I was excited the moment I heard about *React.js Essentials* and even more excited about getting my hands on a copy.

Artemij Fedosejev, a veteran web developer and technical lead at a start-up company in London, demonstrates why a declarative programming style and one-way reactive data flow is often the best way to solve real-life programming problems. Whether you're working with consumer-facing applications or university research, React.js helps you build frontend UIs on both small and large scales. You'll never be lost in code again. Learn from Artemij's real-world experience in *React.js Essentials*, and you'll be creating user interfaces without increasing the complexity of your web application in no time.

This book has everything you need to get started with React.js. It guides you from the first steps down to the intricacies of Jest. The best way to learn is by doing, and throughout this book, you will work on a hands-on React.js project and learn how to build an application that receives and collects the latest photos from Twitter.

Software is constantly evolving and always moving forward. As developers, while practicing our craft, we always reach out to new horizons that stretch and improve our understanding of how great software should be built. Historically, software development and architecture has gone from structured programming to imperative programming. This made way for object-oriented programming (OOP) to become the de facto standard of software development today. Languages such as Java, Ruby, Objective-C, and many others have been built with the OOP paradigm in mind.

However, there was one rebel that embraced functional programming and it has gone down its own evolutionary path, which is JavaScript. React.js is a manifestation of this renewed way of thinking: "UI as a function of state." Facebook has put in a lot of effort into making the reactive approach accessible to us through its library. Unlike other popular frameworks that use templating systems, such as Ember.js and Angular.js, React.js is a UI library that uses a declarative style of programming to describe the UI state. You can think of React.js as the V in the conventional MVC architecture pattern, but it doesn't stop there. Facebook introduced Flux, a complementary application architecture that uses React's composable view components.

The latest approaches to solving programming problems have come full circle and are back to declarative programming. The rise of new paradigms, such as Reactive Extensions (Rx), Futures, and Promises, brings us back to thinking in terms of functions and using a declarative approach instead of OOP's imperative style. React.js incorporates some of these paradigms and *React.js Essentials* is your first step down this path, and I think you'll like where it takes you!

Alex Bush
Founder and Software Product Engineer at SmartCloud, Inc.

About the Author

Artemij Fedosejev is a technical lead living in London, United Kingdom. He is a self-taught web developer who has been a web developer since the early 2000s. Artemij earned his BSc in computer science from University College Cork, Ireland. He participated in the IGNITE Graduate Business Innovation Programme, where he built and launched a website that received the Most Innovative Project award.

After graduation, Artemij moved to London to help local start-up companies build their products. He worked with JavaScript, Node.js, HTML5, CSS3, and other modern web technologies. After gaining some experience in the start-up industry, Artemij was presented with an opportunity to join Imperial College, London, work on a research and development, project and take leadership in creating frontends for a couple of web applications in the public health space. He played a key role in creating frontend architecture using React.js and Flux for WGSA.net and Microreact. org. Artemij created a number of open source projects such as Snapkite Engine, Snapkite Stream Client, and other projects, which can be found on his GitHub account at `https://github.com/fedosejev`. He is also the author of the `http://react.tips` website.

I am deeply grateful to my family, who have always supported me in my efforts. With their love and dedication, I have always been able to focus on learning new things and, now, teaching them to others. Special thanks to Alex Bush for constantly expanding the way I think about software development. Also, this book would have been much harder to write without the support of Dr. David Aanensen and Mirko Menegazzo. And finally, I would like to thank my editors and the wonderful people at Packt Publishing for giving me the opportunity to share my knowledge and experience with other developers around the world.

About the Reviewers

Denis Radin is a frontend engineer working on embedded JavaScript in Liberty Global (Ziggo, UPC). He is passionate about UI experiments and performance optimization. He can be found launching JavaScript into space and the stratosphere in his spare time and believes that this is the sunrise of an interactive revolution. Denis maintains a blog at `http://pixelscommander.com`.

Konstantin Tarkus is a senior software engineer and technology mentor from St. Petersburg, Russia. He specializes in developing web and cloud applications, regularly contributes to the open source community (see the React Starter Kit and Babel Starter Kit projects on GitHub), and enjoys learning new technologies every day. You can find more information about him and reach out to him at `www.codementor.io/koistya`.

www.PacktPub.com

Support files, eBooks, discount offers, and more

For support files and downloads related to your book, please visit www.PacktPub.com.

Did you know that Packt offers eBook versions of every book published, with PDF and ePub files available? You can upgrade to the eBook version at www.PacktPub.com and as a print book customer, you are entitled to a discount on the eBook copy. Get in touch with us at service@packtpub.com for more details.

At www.PacktPub.com, you can also read a collection of free technical articles, sign up for a range of free newsletters and receive exclusive discounts and offers on Packt books and eBooks.

https://www2.packtpub.com/books/subscription/packtlib

Do you need instant solutions to your IT questions? PacktLib is Packt's online digital book library. Here, you can search, access, and read Packt's entire library of books.

Why subscribe?

- Fully searchable across every book published by Packt
- Copy and paste, print, and bookmark content
- On demand and accessible via a web browser

Free access for Packt account holders

If you have an account with Packt at www.PacktPub.com, you can use this to access PacktLib today and view 9 entirely free books. Simply use your login credentials for immediate access.

Table of Contents

Preface

Today, the Web is different. The way we build for the Web is different. Faced by the challenges of dealing with unmaintainable imperative code produced by jQuery we had to look for new ways of managing the complexity of modern user interfaces. We needed a new user interface library that would help us build declarative, modular, fast, and scalable frontend applications
using JavaScript.

Meet React.js — a JavaScript user interface library developed by Facebook. It brings profound ideas on how to work with the DOM, organize your application's data flow, and think about user interface elements as individual components. And yet, it's only a user interface library that makes no assumptions about the rest of your technology stack.

Combined with Flux, we get a powerful frontend architecture that makes sense not only to experienced developers, but also to those who're just starting their frontend journey.

Dear frontend developers of all experience levels, solving all kind of business challenges, in teams of all sizes with deadlines of all urgency levels... welcome to a better future!

Get ready to be surprised by the simplicity, predictability, and thoughtfulness of React.js.

What this book covers

Chapter 1, Installing Powerful Tools for Your Project, outlines the goal of this book and explains what modern tools you need to install in order to build React applications efficiently. It introduces each tool and provides step-by-step instructions on how to install each of them. Then, it creates a structure for the project that we'll be building in this book.

Chapter 2, Create Your First React Element, explains how to install React and introduces virtual DOM. Then, it explains what React Element is and how to create and render one with native JavaScript syntax. Finally, it introduces the JSX syntax and shows how to create React Elements using JSX.

Chapter 3, Create Your First React Component, introduces React components. It explains the difference between stateless and stateful React components and how to decide which one to use. Then, it guides you through the process of creating both kinds.

Chapter 4, Make Your React Components Reactive, explains how to solve a problem with React and walks you through the process of planning your React application. It creates a React component that encapsulates the entire React application that we build in this book. It explains the relationship between parent and child React components.

Chapter 5, Use Your React Components with Another Library, explores how to use third-party JavaScript libraries with your React components. It introduces React component's lifecycle, demonstrates how to use mounting methods, and creates new React components for our book's project.

Chapter 6, Update Your React Components, introduces React component lifecycle's updating methods. This covers how to use CSS styles in JavaScript. It explains how to validate and set the default component's properties.

Chapter 7, Build Complex React Components, focuses on building more complex React components. It explores the details of how to implement different React components and how to put them together into one coherent and fully functional React application.

Chapter 8, Test Your React Application with Jest, explains the idea of unit testing and how to write and run your unit tests with Jest. It also demonstrates how to test your React components. It discusses test suites, specs, expectations, and matchers.

Chapter 9, Supercharge Your React Architecture with Flux, discusses how to improve the architecture of our React application. It introduces the Flux architecture and explains the role of dispatcher, stores, and action creators.

Chapter 10, Prepare Your React Application for Painless Maintenance with Flux, explains how to decouple concerns in your React application with Flux. It refactors our React application to allow painless maintainability in the future.

What you need for this book

First of all, you need the latest version of a modern web browser, such as Google Chrome or Mozilla Firefox:

- Google Chrome: `https://www.google.com/chrome/browser`
- Mozilla Firefox: `https://www.mozilla.org/en-US/firefox/new/`

Second, you will need to install Git, Node.js, and npm. You will find detailed instructions on how to install and use them in *Chapter 1, Installing Powerful Tools for Your Project*.

Finally, you will need a code editor. I recommend Sublime Text (`http://www.sublimetext.com`). Alternatively, you can use Atom (`https://atom.io`), Brackets (`http://brackets.io`), Visual Studio Code (`https://code.visualstudio.com`), or any other editor of your preference.

Who this book is for

This book is intended for frontend developers who want to build scalable and maintainable user interfaces for the Web. Some core knowledge of JavaScript, HTML, and CSS is the only thing you need to know to start benefiting from the revolutionary ideas that React.js brings into the web development world. If you have previous experience with jQuery or Angular.js, then you will benefit from understanding how React.js is different and how to take advantage of integrating different libraries with it.

Conventions

In this book, you will find a number of text styles that distinguish between different kinds of information. Here are some examples of these styles and an explanation of their meaning.

Code words in text, database table names, folder names, filenames, file extensions, pathnames, dummy URLs, user input, and Twitter handles are shown as follows: "The entry point to the React library is the `React` object."

A block of code is set as follows:

```
var React = require('react');
var ReactDOM = require('react-dom');
var reactElement = React.createElement(
  'h1',
  { className: 'header' }
);
ReactDOM.render(
  reactElement,
  document.getElementById('react-application')
);
```

When we wish to draw your attention to a particular part of a code block, the relevant lines or items are set in bold:

```
<!doctype html>
<html lang="en">
  <head>
    <title>Snapterest</title>
  </head>
  <body>
    <div id="react-application">
      I am about to learn the essentials of React.js.
    </div>
    <script src="./snapterest.js"></script>
  </body>
</html>
```

Any command-line input or output is written as follows:

```
cd ~
git clone https://github.com/snapkite/snapkite-engine.git
```

New terms and **important words** are shown in bold. Words that you see on the screen, for example, in menus or dialog boxes, appear in the text like this: "You should see the following text: **I am about to learn the essentials of React.js.**"

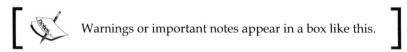

Warnings or important notes appear in a box like this.

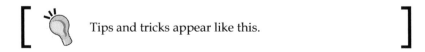

Tips and tricks appear like this.

Reader feedback

Feedback from our readers is always welcome. Let us know what you think about this book—what you liked or disliked. Reader feedback is important for us as it helps us develop titles that you will really get the most out of.

To send us general feedback, simply e-mail feedback@packtpub.com, and mention the book's title in the subject of your message.

If there is a topic that you have expertise in and you are interested in either writing or contributing to a book, see our author guide at www.packtpub.com/authors.

Customer support

Now that you are the proud owner of a Packt book, we have a number of things to help you to get the most from your purchase.

Downloading the example code

You can download the example code files from your account at http://www.packtpub.com for all the Packt Publishing books you have purchased. If you purchased this book elsewhere, you can visit http://www.packtpub.com/support and register to have the files e-mailed directly to you.

For this book, the source code files can be downloaded or forked from the following GitHub repository as well: https://github.com/fedosejev/react-essentials

Errata

Although we have taken every care to ensure the accuracy of our content, mistakes do happen. If you find a mistake in one of our books—maybe a mistake in the text or the code—we would be grateful if you could report this to us. By doing so, you can save other readers from frustration and help us improve subsequent versions of this book. If you find any errata, please report them by visiting http://www.packtpub.com/submit-errata, selecting your book, clicking on the **Errata Submission Form** link, and entering the details of your errata. Once your errata are verified, your submission will be accepted and the errata will be uploaded to our website or added to any list of existing errata under the Errata section of that title.

To view the previously submitted errata, go to https://www.packtpub.com/books/content/support and enter the name of the book in the search field. The required information will appear under the **Errata** section.

Piracy

Piracy of copyrighted material on the Internet is an ongoing problem across all media. At Packt, we take the protection of our copyright and licenses very seriously. If you come across any illegal copies of our works in any form on the Internet, please provide us with the location address or website name immediately so that we can pursue a remedy.

Please contact us at copyright@packtpub.com with a link to the suspected pirated material.

We appreciate your help in protecting our authors and our ability to bring you valuable content.

Questions

If you have a problem with any aspect of this book, you can contact us at questions@packtpub.com, and we will do our best to address the problem. You can also create a new issue on GitHub repository for this book at https://github.com/fedosejev/react-essentials/issues.

1
Installing Powerful Tools for Your Project

Here is a great quote by Charles F. Kettering:

My interest is in the future because I am going to spend the rest of my life there.

This brilliant inventor has left software engineers with the single most important piece of advice way before we even started thinking how to write software. Yet, half a century later, we're still figuring out why we end up with spaghetti code or the "spaghetti mental model".

Have you ever been in a situation where you inherit code from a previous developer and spend weeks trying to understand how everything works because no blueprints were made available, and the pseudo-self-explanatory-code became too hard to debug? Better yet, the project keeps growing and so does its complexity. Making breaking changes is dangerous and no one wants to touch that "ugly" legacy code. Rewriting the whole codebase is way too expensive, so the current one is supported by introducing new bug fixes and patches every day. It is a well-known fact that the cost of maintaining software is way higher than the original cost of developing it.

What does it mean to write software for the future, today? I think it boils down to creating a simple mental model that doesn't change, no matter how big your project becomes over time. When the size of your project grows, the complexity always stays the same. This mental model is your blueprint, and once you understand it you will understand how your whole piece of software works.

If you take a look at modern web development, and in particular, the frontend development, you'll notice that we live in exciting times. Internet companies and individual developers are tackling problems of speed and cost of development versus code and user experience quality.

In 2013, Facebook released React—an open source JavaScript library for building user interfaces. You can read more about it at `http://facebook.github.io/react/`. In early 2015, Tom Occhino from Facebook summarized what makes React so powerful:

> *React wraps an imperative API with a declarative one. React's real power lies in how it makes you to write code.*

Most of you know that a declarative style of programming results in less code. It tells a computer what to do without specifying how, while an imperative style of programming describes how to do it. JavaScript's call to the DOM API is an example of imperative programming. jQuery is another such example.

Facebook used React in production for years, along with Instagram and other companies. It works for small projects too; here is an example of a shopping list built with React: `http://fedosejev.github.io/shopping-list-react`. I think React is one of the best JavaScript libraries used for building user interfaces that is available for developers today.

My goal is for you to understand the fundamental principles of React. To achieve this, I will introduce you to one React concept at a time, explain it, and show how you can apply it. Step by step we'll build a real-time web application, raise important questions along the way, and discuss solutions that React provides us with.

We will learn about Flux, which implements a unidirectional flow of data. Together with Flux and React, we'll create a predictable and manageable code base that you will be able to expand by adding new features, without scaling its complexity. The mental model of how your web application works will stay the same no matter how many new features you add later on.

As with any new technology, there are things that work very differently from the way that you're used to. React is not an exception. In fact, some of the core concepts of React might look counter-intuitive, thought provoking, or even a step backward. Don't rush to any conclusions. As you would expect, there are very good reasons behind how React works, and these reasons come from experienced Facebook engineers who build and use React in production in business-critical applications. My advice to you is to keep your mind open while learning React, and I believe that, at the end of this book, these new concepts will settle in and make great sense to you.

Please join me in this journey of learning React and following Charles F. Kettering's advice. Let's take care of our future!

Approaching our project

I firmly believe that the best motivation for learning new technology is a project that excites you and that you can't wait to build. As an experienced developer, you've probably already built a number of successful commercial projects that share certain product features, design patterns, and even target audiences. In this book, I want you to build a project that feels like a breath of fresh air. A project which you most likely wouldn't build in your day-to-day work. It has to be a fun endeavor, which not only educates you but also satisfies your curiosity and stretches your imagination. Yet, guessing that you're a busy professional, this project shouldn't be a time consuming, long-term commitment for you either.

Enter **Snapterest**—a web application that allows you to discover and collect public photos posted on Twitter. Think of it as Pinterest (`www.pinterest.com`) with the only source of pictures being Twitter. We will implement a fully functional website with the following core functionalities:

- Receiving and displaying tweets in real time
- Adding and removing tweets to/from a collection
- Reviewing collected tweets
- Exporting a collection of tweets as an HTML snippet that you can share

When you start working on a new project, the very first thing that you do is you get your tools ready. For this project, we will be using a number of tools that you might not be familiar with, so let's discuss what they are, and how you can install and configure them.

If you have any trouble with installing and configuring the tools and modules from this chapter, then go to `https://github.com/fedosejev/react-essentials` and create a new issue; describe what you're doing and what error message you're getting. I will do my best to help you resolve your issue.

In this book, I'll assume that you're working on a Macintosh or Windows computer. If you're a Unix user, then most likely you will know your package manager very well, and it should be easy enough for you to install the tools that you will learn about in this chapter.

Let's start with the installation of Node.js.

Installing Node.js and npm

Node.js (`https://nodejs.org`) is a platform that allows us to write server-side applications with a client-side language that we're all familiar with—JavaScript. However, the real benefit of Node.js is that it uses an event-driven, non-blocking I/O model, which is perfect for building data-intensive, real-time applications. It means that, with Node.js, we should be able to handle an incoming stream of tweets and process them as soon as they arrive: just what we need for our project.

Let's install Node.js. We'll be using version v0.10.40 because, at the time of writing this book, that's the latest version of Node.js that Jest supports. Jest is a testing framework from Facebook that you'll learn about in *Chapter 8, Test Your React Application with Jest*.

Go to `http://nodejs.org/dist/v0.10.40/` and download the installation package for your OS:

- OS X: `http://nodejs.org/dist/v0.10.40/node-v0.10.40.pkg`
- Windows 64-bit: `http://nodejs.org/dist/v0.10.40/x64/node-v0.10.40-x64.msi`
- Windows 32-bit: `http://nodejs.org/dist/v0.10.40/node-v0.10.40-x86.msi`

Run it and follow the installation steps that Node.js will prompt you with. Once finished, check whether you have successfully installed Node.js. Open Terminal/ Command Prompt, and type the following command:

```
node -v
```

The output is as follows:

```
v0.10.40
```

Node.js has a very rich ecosystem of modules that is available for us to use. A module is a Node.js application that you can reuse in your own Node.js application. At the time of writing, there are over 120,000 modules. How do you manage such a wide diversity of Node.js modules? Meet **npm**, a package manager that manages Node.js modules. In fact, npm is shipped together with Node.js, so you've got it installed already. Type in your Terminal/Command Prompt:

```
npm -v
```

You should see the following output:

`1.4.28`

You can learn more about npm at `www.npmjs.com`. Now we are ready to start with the installation of Node.js applications.

Installing Git

In this book, we'll be using Git to install Node.js modules. If you haven't installed Git yet, visit `https://git-scm.com/book/en/v2/Getting-Started-Installing-Git` and follow the installation instructions for your OS.

Getting data from the Twitter Streaming API

The data for our React application will come from Twitter. Twitter has the **Streaming API** that anyone can plug into and start receiving an endless flow of public tweets in the JSON format.

To start using the Twitter Streaming API, you'll need to perform the following steps:

1. Create a Twitter account. For this, go to `https://twitter.com` and sign up; or sign in if you already have an account.

2. Create a new Twitter App by navigating to `https://apps.twitter.com`, and click on **Create New App**. You will need to fill in the **Application Details** form, agree with the **Developer Agreement**, and click on **Create your Twitter application**. Now you should see your application's page. Switch to the **Keys and Access Tokens** tab.

In the **Application Settings** section of this page, you'll find two vital pieces of information:

*   **Consumer Key (API Key)**; for example, `jqRDrAlKQCbCbu2o4iclpnvem`
*   **Consumer Secret (API Secret)**; for example, `wJcdogJih7uLpjzcs2JtAvdSyCVlqHIRUWI70aHOAf7E3wWIgD`

Take a note of them; we will need them later in this chapter.

Now we need to generate an access token. On the same page, you'll see **Your Access Token** section that is empty. Click on **Create my access token**. It creates two pieces of information:

- **Access Token**; for example,
  `12736172-R017ah2pE2OCtmi46IAE2n0z3u2DV6IqsEcPa0THR`

- **Access Token Secret**; for example,
  `4RTJJWIezIDcs5VX1PMVZolXGZG7L3Ez7Iz1gMdZucDaM`

Take a note of them too. An access token is unique to you and you should not share it with anyone. Keep it private.

Now we have everything that we need to start using Twitter's Streaming API.

Filtering data with Snapkite Engine

The amount of tweets that you'll receive via the Twitter Streaming API is more than you can ever consume, so we need to find a way to filter that stream of data into a meaningful set of tweets that we can display and interact with. I recommend that you take a quick look at the Twitter Streaming API documentation at https://dev.twitter.com/streaming, and in particular, take a look at this page that describes the way you can filter an incoming stream at https://dev.twitter.com/streaming/reference/post/statuses/filter. You'll notice that Twitter provides very few filters that we can apply, so we need to find a way to filter that stream of data even further.

Luckily, there is a Node.js application just for this. It's called **Snapkite Engine**. It connects to the Twitter Streaming API, filters it using the available filters and according to the rules that you define, and outputs the filtered tweets to a web socket connection. Our proposed React application can listen to the events on that socket connection and process tweets as they arrive.

Let's install Snapkite Engine.

First, you need to clone the Snapkite Engine repository. Cloning means that you're copying the source code from a GitHub server to your local directory. In this book, I'll assume that your local directory is your home directory. Open Terminal/Command Prompt and type the following commands:

```
cd ~
```

```
git clone https://github.com/snapkite/snapkite-engine.git
```

This should create the ~/snapkite-engine/ folder. We're now going to install all the other node modules that snapkite-engine depends on. One of them is the node-gyp module. Depending on what platform you're using, Unix or Windows, you will need to install other tools that are listed on this web page: https://github.com/TooTallNate/node-gyp#installation.

Once you install them, you're ready to install the node-gyp module:

```
npm install --global node-gyp
```

Now navigate to the ~/snapkite-engine directory:

```
cd snapkite-engine/
```

Then run the following command:

```
npm install
```

This command will install the Node.js modules that Snapkite Engine depends on. Now let's configure Snapkite Engine. Assuming that you're in the ~/snapkite-engine/ directory, copy the ./example.config.json file to ./config.json by running the following command:

```
cp example.config.json config.json
```

Or if you're using Windows, run this command:

```
copy example.config.json config.json
```

Open config.json in your favorite text editor. We will now edit the configuration properties. Let's start with trackKeywords. This is where we will tell what keywords we want to track. If we want to track the keyword "my", then set it as follows:

```
    "trackKeywords": "my"
```

Next, we need to set our Twitter Streaming API keys. Set consumerKey, consumerSecret, accessTokenKey, and accessTokenSecret to the keys you saved when you created your Twitter App. Other properties can be set to their defaults. If you're curious to learn about what they are, check out the Snapkite Engine documentation at https://github.com/snapkite/snapkite-engine.

Our next step is to install Snapkite Filters. **Snapkite Filter** is a Node.js module that validates tweets according to a set of rules. There are a number of Snapkite Filters out there, and we can use any combination of them to filter our stream of tweets as we like. You can find a list of all the available Snapkite Filters at https://github.com/snapkite/snapkite-filters.

In our application, we'll use the following Snapkite Filters:

- **Is Possibly Sensitive**: https://github.com/snapkite/snapkite-filter-is-possibly-sensitive
- **Has Mobile Photo**: https://github.com/snapkite/snapkite-filter-has-mobile-photo
- **Is Retweet**: https://github.com/snapkite/snapkite-filter-is-retweet
- **Has Text**: https://github.com/snapkite/snapkite-filter-has-text

Let's install them. Navigate to the ~/snapkite-engine/filters/ directory:

```
cd ~/snapkite-engine/filters/
```

Then clone all Snapkite Filters by running these commands:

```
git clone https://github.com/snapkite/snapkite-filter-is-possibly-sensitive.git
git clone https://github.com/snapkite/snapkite-filter-has-mobile-photo.git
git clone https://github.com/snapkite/snapkite-filter-is-retweet.git
git clone https://github.com/snapkite/snapkite-filter-has-text.git
```

The next step is to configure them. In order to do so, you need to create a configuration file for each Snapkite Filter in **JSON** format and define some properties in it. Luckily, each Snapkite Filter comes with an example configuration file that we can duplicate and edit as needed. Assuming that you're in the ~/snapkite-engine/filters/ directory, run the following commands (use copy and replace the forward slashes with the backward slashes on Windows):

```
cp snapkite-filter-is-possibly-sensitive/example.config.json snapkite-filter-is-possibly-sensitive/config.json
cp snapkite-filter-has-mobile-photo/example.config.json snapkite-filter-has-mobile-photo/config.json
cp snapkite-filter-is-retweet/example.config.json snapkite-filter-is-retweet/config.json
cp snapkite-filter-has-text/example.config.json snapkite-filter-has-text/config.json
```

We don't need to change any of the default settings in these config.json files, as they're already configured to fit our purposes.

Finally, we need to tell Snapkite Engine which Snapkite Filters it should use. Open the `~/snapkite-engine/config.json` file in a text editor and look for this:

```
"filters": []
```

Now replace that with the following:

```
"filters": [
  "snapkite-filter-is-possibly-sensitive",
  "snapkite-filter-has-mobile-photo",
  "snapkite-filter-is-retweet",
  "snapkite-filter-has-text"
]
```

Well done! You've successfully installed Snapkite Engine with a number of Snapkite Filters. Now let's check if we can run it. Navigate to `~/snapkite-engine/` and run the following command:

npm start

You should see no error messages, but if you do and you're not sure how to fix them, then please go to `https://github.com/fedosejev/react-essentials/issues`, create a new issue and copy/paste the error message that you get.

Next, let's set up our project's structure.

Creating the project structure

It's time to create our project structure. Organizing source files may sound like a simple task, but a well-thought-out project structure organization helps us understand the underlying architecture of our application. You'll see an example of this later in this book, when we'll talk about the Flux application architecture. Let's start by creating our root project directory named `snapterest` inside your home directory `~/snapterest/`.

Then, inside it, we will create two other directories:

- `~/snapterest/source/`: Here we'll store our source JavaScript files
- `~/snapterest/build/`: Here we'll put compiled JavaScript files and an HTML file.

Now, inside `~/snapterest/source/`, create the `components/` folder so that your project structure would look like this:

- `~/snapterest/source/components/`
- `~/snapterest/build/`

Now, when we have our fundamental project structure ready, let's start populating it with our application files. First, we need to create our main application file `app.js` in the `~/snapterest/source/` directory. This file will be the entry point to our application, `~/snapterest/source/app.js`.

Leave it empty for now, as we have a more pressing matter to discuss.

Creating package.json

Have you ever heard of **DRY** before? It stands for **Don't Repeat Yourself,** and it promotes one of the core principles in software development — code reuse. The best code is the one that you don't need to write. In fact, one of our goals in this project is to write as little code as possible. You might not realize this just yet, but React helps us achieve this goal. Not only does it save us time, but if we also decide to maintain and improve our project in future, it will save us even more time in the long run.

When it comes to not writing code, we can apply the following strategies:

- Writing our code in a declarative programming style
- Reusing the code written by someone else

In this project, we'll be using both these techniques. The first one is covered by React itself. React leaves us no choice but to write our JavaScript code in a declarative style. This means that instead of telling our web browser how to do what we want (like we do in jQuery), we just tell it what we want it to do and the how part is explained by React. That's a win for us.

Node.js and npm cover the second technique. I've mentioned earlier in this chapter that there are a hundred thousand different Node.js applications available for us to use. This means that most likely someone has already implemented the functionality that our application depends on.

The question is how do you know from where to get all these Node.js applications that we want to reuse. We can install them via the `npm install <package-name>` command. In the npm context, a Node.js application is called a **package**, and each **npm package** has a `package.json` file that describes the metadata associated with that package. You can learn more about what fields are stored in `package.json` at `https://docs.npmjs.com/files/package.json`.

Before we install our dependency packages, we will initialize a package for our own project. Normally, `package.json` is only required when you want to submit your package to the npm registry so that others can reuse your Node.js application. We're not going to build a Node.js application, and we're not going to submit our project to npm. Remember that `package.json` is technically only a metadata file that the npm command understands, and as such, we can use it to store a list of dependencies that our application requires. Once we store a list of dependencies in `package.json`, we can easily install them anytime with the `npm install` command; npm will figure out from where to get them automatically.

How do we create the `package.json` file for our own application? Luckily, npm comes with an interactive tool that asks us a bunch of questions and then, based on our answers, creates `package.json` for our project.

Make sure that you're located in the `~/snapterest/` directory. On the Terminal/Command Prompt run the following command:

```
npm init
```

The first question it will ask you is your package name. It will suggest a default name that is the directory name you're located in. It should suggest `name: (snapterest)` in our case. Press *Enter* to accept the proposed default name (`snapterest`). The next question is the version of your package, that is, `version: (1.0.0)`. Press *Enter*. These two would be the most important fields if we were planning to submit our package to npm for others to reuse. Because we're not going to submit it to npm, we can confidently accept defaults for all the questions that we are asked. Keep pressing *Enter* until `npm init` completes its execution and exits. Then, if you go to your `~/snapterest/` directory, you will find a new file there, `package.json`.

Now we're ready to install other Node.js applications that we're going to reuse. An application that is built of multiple individual applications is called modular, whereas individual applications are called modules. This is what we'll call our Node.js dependencies from now on — Node.js modules.

Reusing Node.js modules

As I mentioned earlier, there will be a step in our development process called building. During this step, our build script will take our source files and all our Node.js dependency packages, and transform them into a single file that web browsers can successfully execute. The most important part of this building process is called packaging. But what do we need to package and why? Let's think about it. I briefly mentioned earlier that we're not creating a Node.js application, but yet we're talking about reusing Node.js modules. Does this mean that we'll be reusing Node.js modules in a non-Node.js application? Is that even possible? Turns out, there is a way of doing that.

Browserify is a tool used for bundling all your dependency files together in such a way that you can reuse Node.js modules in client-side JavaScript applications. You can learn more about Browserify at `http://browserify.org`. To install Browserify, run the following command from inside the `~/snapterest/` directory:

```
npm install --save-dev browserify
```

Notice the `--save-dev` flag. It tells npm to add Browserify to our `package.json` as a development dependency. Adding a module name to our `package.json` file as a dependency allows us to record what dependencies we're using, and we can easily install them later with the `npm install` command, if needed. There is a distinction between dependencies that are required to run your application and the ones that are required to develop your application. Browserify is used at build time, and not at runtime, so it's a development dependency. Hence the use of the `--save-dev` flag. If you check the content of your `package.json` file now, you'll see this:

```
"devDependencies": {
    "browserify": "^11.0.1"
}
```

Notice that npm created a new folder in your `~/snapterest/` directory called `node_modules`. This is the place where it puts all your local dependency modules.

Congrats on installing your first Node.js module! Browserify will allow us to use Node.js modules in our client-side JavaScript applications. It will be a part of our build process. Speaking of which, I think it's a good time to introduce you to our build tools.

Building with Gulp.js

Today, any modern client-side application represents a mix of many concerns that are addressed individually by various technologies. Addressing each concern individually simplifies the overall process of managing the project's complexity. The downside of this approach is that at some point in your project, you need to put together all the individual parts into one coherent application. Just like the robots in an automotive factory that assemble cars from individual parts, developers have something called build-tools that assemble their projects from individual modules. This process is called the **build** process and, depending on the size and complexity of your project, it can take anywhere from milliseconds to hours to build.

The Node.js ecosystem has a great tool for automating our build process, **Gulp.js**. You can learn more about Gulp.js at `http://gulpjs.com`. Let's install it:

```
npm install --save-dev gulp
```

Once again, we need this module for developing, but not running, our application. Only this time we also want to install our module globally:

```
npm install --global gulp
```

This would allow us to run it from the Terminal/Command Prompt. To check whether you have Gulp.js installed, run this command:

```
gulp
```

You should see the following output:

```
No gulpfile found
```

This means that you have successfully installed Gulp.js.

What is this **gulpfile** anyway? It's a file where we describe our build process. Create gulpfile.js in your ~/snapterest/ directory and add the following content to it:

```
var gulp = require('gulp');

gulp.task('default', function() {
  console.log('I am about to learn the essentials of React.js');
});
```

Now if you run the gulp command, you will see output that looks like this:

```
Using gulpfile ~/snapterest/gulpfile.js
Starting 'default'...
I am about to learn the essentials of React.js
Finished 'default' after 62 µs
```

By default, when you run gulp, it executes a task called (no surprise here) default. Well done! You now have a working Gulp.js build system. Let's create a task that will package our source and dependency modules using Browserify.

Replace the content of your gulpfile.js with the following code:

```
var gulp = require('gulp');
var browserify = require('browserify');
var babelify = require('babelify');
var source = require('vinyl-source-stream');

gulp.task('default', function () {
  return browserify('./source/app.js')
        .transform(babelify)
```

```
      .bundle()
      .pipe(source('snapterest.js'))
      .pipe(gulp.dest('./build/'));
});
```

As you can see, we will use the `require()` function to import three new dependency modules: `browserify`, `babelify`, and `vinyl-source-stream`. We have already installed the `browserify` module, so now let's install the `babelify` module:

npm install --save-dev babelify

The `babelify` module allows us to write the JSX syntax that we'll introduce in the next chapter.

Why do we need the `vinyl-source-stream` module? In a nutshell, it allows us to use Browserify and Gulp together. If you're interested in more details on why this works, go to `https://www.npmjs.com/package/vinyl-source-stream`. Let's install our `vinyl-source-stream` dependency module:

npm install --save-dev vinyl-source-stream

Now we're ready to test our `default` task. Run this command:

gulp

The output should look something like this:

Using gulpfile ~/snapterest/gulpfile.js

Starting 'default'...

Finished 'default' after 48 ms

More importantly, if you check your project's ~/snapterest/build/ directory, you'll notice that it now has the `snapterest.js` file with some code already inside it—that's our (empty) JavaScript application with some Node.js modules that are ready to run in a web browser!

Creating a web page

If you're starving for some React goodness, then I have great news for you! We're almost there. All that's left to do is to create `index.html` with a link to our `snapterest.js` script.

Create the `index.html` file in the `~/snapterest/build/` directory. Add the following HTML markup to it:

```html
<!doctype html>
<html lang="en">
  <head>
    <meta charset="utf-8" />
    <meta http-equiv="x-ua-compatible" content="ie=edge, chrome=1" />
    <title>Snapterest</title>
    <link rel="stylesheet" href="https://maxcdn.bootstrapcdn.com/
bootstrap/3.3.5/css/bootstrap.min.css">
  </head>
  <body>
    <div id="react-application">
      I am about to learn the essentials of React.js.
    </div>
    <script src="./snapterest.js"></script>
  </body>
</html>
```

Open `~/snapterest/build/index.html` in a web browser. You should see the following text: **I am about to learn the essentials of React.js**. That's right, we have finished setting up our project, and it's time to get to know React!

Summary

In this chapter, we learned why we should use React to build user interfaces for modern web applications. Then, we discussed the project that we'll be building in this book. Finally, we installed all the right tools and created the project's structure. In the next chapter, we'll install React, take a closer look at how React works, and create our first React Element.

2
Create Your First React Element

As many of you know, creating a simple web application today involves writing the HTML, CSS, and JavaScript code. The reason we use three different technologies is because we want to separate three different concerns:

- Content (HTML)
- Styling (CSS)
- Logic (JavaScript)

This separation works great for creating a web page because, traditionally, we had different people working on different parts of our web page: one person structured the content using HTML and styled it using CSS, and then another person implemented the dynamic behavior of various elements on that web page using JavaScript. It was a content-centric approach.

Today, we mostly don't think of a website as a collection of web pages anymore. Instead, we build web applications that might have only one web page, and that web page does not represent the layout for our content—it represents a container for our web application. Such a web application with a single web page is called (unsurprisingly) a **Single Page Application** (**SPA**). You might be wondering, how do we represent the rest of the content in a SPA? Surely, we need to create an additional layout using HTML tags? Otherwise, how does a web browser know what to render?

These are all valid questions. Let's take a look at how it works. Once you load your web page in a web browser, it creates a **Document Object Model (DOM)** of that web page. A DOM represents your web page in a tree structure, and at this point, it reflects the structure of the layout that you created with only HTML tags. This is what happens regardless of whether you're building a traditional web page or a SPA. The difference between the two is what happens next. If you are building a traditional web page, then you would finish creating your web page's layout. On the other hand, if you are building a SPA, then you would need to start creating additional elements by manipulating the DOM with JavaScript. A web browser provides you with the **JavaScript DOM API** to do this. You can learn more about it at `https://developer.mozilla.org/en-US/docs/Web/API/Document_Object_Model`.

However, manipulating (or mutating) the DOM with JavaScript has two issues:

- Your programming style will be imperative if you decide to use the JavaScript DOM API directly. As we discussed in the previous chapter, this programming style leads to a code base that is harder to maintain.

- DOM mutations are slow because they cannot be optimized for speed, unlike other JavaScript code.

Luckily, React solves both these problems for us.

Understanding the virtual DOM

Why do we need to manipulate the DOM in the first place? Because our web applications are not static. They have a state represented by the **user interface (UI)** that a web browser renders, and that state can be changed when an event occurs. What kind of events are we talking about? There are two types of events that we're interested in:

- User events: When a user types, clicks, scrolls, resizes, and so on
- Server events: When an application receives data or an error from a server, among others

What happens while handling these events? Usually, we update the data that our application depends on, and that data represents a state of our data model. In turn, when a state of our data model changes, we might want to reflect this change by updating a state of our UI. Looks like what we want is a way of syncing two different states: the UI state and the data model state. We want one to react to the changes in the other and vice versa. How can we achieve this?

One of the ways to sync your application's UI state with an underlying data model's state is two-way data binding. There are different types of two-way data binding. One of them is key-value observing (KVO), which is used in Ember.js, Knockout, Backbone, and iOS, among others. Another one is dirty checking, which is used in Angular.

Instead of two-way data binding, React offers a different solution called the **virtual DOM**. The virtual DOM is a fast, in-memory representation of the real DOM, and it's an abstraction that allows us to treat JavaScript and DOM as if they were reactive. Let's take a look at how it works:

1. Whenever the state of your data model changes, the virtual DOM and React will rerender your UI to a virtual DOM representation.

2. React then calculates the difference between the two virtual DOM representations: the previous virtual DOM representation that was computed before the data was changed and the current virtual DOM representation that was computed after the data was changed. This difference between the two virtual DOM representations is what actually needs to be changed in the real DOM.

3. React updates only what needs to be updated in the real DOM.

The process of finding a difference between the two representations of the virtual DOM and rerendering only the updated patches in a real DOM is fast. Also, the best part is, as a React developer, that you don't need to worry about what actually needs to be rerendered. React allows you to write your code as if you were rerendering the entire DOM every time your application's state changes.

If you would like to learn more about the virtual DOM, the rationale behind it, and how it can be compared to data binding, then I would strongly recommend that you watch this very informative talk by Pete Hunt from Facebook at `https://www.youtube.com/watch?v=-DX3vJiqxm4`.

Now that we've learnt about the virtual DOM, let's mutate a real DOM by installing React and creating our first React element.

Installing React

To start using the React library, we need to first install it. I am going to show you two ways of doing this: the simplest one and the one using the `npm install` command.

The simplest way is to add the `<script>` tag to our `~/snapterest/build/index.html` file:

- For the development version of React, add the following command:

```
<script src="https://cdnjs.cloudflare.com/ajax/libs/react/0.14.0-beta3/react.js"></script>
```

- For the production version version of React, add the following command:

```
<script src="https://cdnjs.cloudflare.com/ajax/libs/react/0.14.0-beta3/react.min.js"></script>
```

There is a difference between the two that we'll learn about in the later chapters of this book. For our project, we'll be using the development version of React.

At the time of writing, the latest version of React library is 0.14.0-beta3. Over time, React gets updated, so make sure you use the latest version that is available to you, unless it introduces breaking changes that are incompatible with the code samples provided in this book. Visit `https://github.com/fedosejev/react-essentials` to learn about any compatibility issues between the code samples and the latest version of React.

In *Chapter 1, Installing Powerful Tools for Your Project*, I introduced you to **Browserify** that allows us to import all the dependency modules for our application using the `require()` function. We'll be using `require()` to import the React library as well, which means that, instead of adding a `<script>` tag to our `index.html`, we'll be using the `npm install` command to install React:

1. Navigate to the `~/snapterest/` directory and run this command:

```
npm install --save react@0.14.0-beta3 react-dom@0.14.0-beta3
```

2. Then, open the `~/snapterest/source/app.js` file in your text editor and import the React and ReactDOM libraries to the `React` and `ReactDOM` variables, respectively:

```
var React = require('react');
var ReactDOM = require('react-dom');
```

The `react` package contains methods that are concerned with the key idea behind React, that is, describing what you want to render in a declarative way. On the other hand, the `react-dom` package offers methods that are responsible for rendering to the DOM. You can read more about why developers at Facebook think it's a good idea to separate the React library into two packages at `https://facebook.github.io/react/blog/2015/07/03/react-v0.14-beta-1.html#two-packages`.

Now we're ready to start using the React library in our project. Next, let's create our first React Element!

Creating React Elements with JavaScript

We'll start by familiarizing ourselves with a fundamental React terminology. It will help us build a clear picture of what the React library is made of. This terminology will most likely update over time, so keep an eye on the official documentation at `http://facebook.github.io/react/docs/glossary.html`.

Just like the DOM is a tree of nodes, React's virtual DOM is a tree of React nodes. One of the core types in React is called `ReactNode`. It's a building block for a virtual DOM, and it can be any one of these core types:

- `ReactElement`: This is the primary type in React. It's a light, stateless, immutable, virtual representation of a DOM `Element`.

- `ReactText`: This is a string or a number. It represents textual content and it's a virtual representation of a Text Node in the DOM.

`ReactElement`s and `ReactText`s are `ReactNode`s. An array of `ReactNode`s is called a `ReactFragment`. You will see examples of all of these in this chapter.

Let's start with an example of a `ReactElement`:

1. Add the following code to your `~/snapterest/source/app.js` file:

```
var reactElement = React.createElement('h1');
ReactDOM.render(reactElement, document.getElementById('react-application'));
```

2. Now your `app.js` file should look exactly like this:

```
var React = require('react');
var ReactDOM = require('react-dom');
var reactElement = React.createElement('h1');
ReactDOM.render(reactElement, document.getElementById('react-application'));
```

3. Navigate to the `~/snapterest/` directory and run Gulp's `default` task:

```
gulp
```

You will see the following output:

```
Starting 'default'...
Finished 'default' after 1.73 s
```

4. Navigate to the `~/snapterest/build/` directory, and open `index.html` in a web browser. You will see a blank web page. Open **Developer Tools** in your web browser and inspect the HTML markup for your blank web page. You should see this line, among others:

```
<h1 data-reactid=".0"></h1>
```

Well done! We've just created your first React element. Let's see exactly how we did it.

The entry point to the React library is the `React` object. This object has a method called `createElement()` that takes three parameters: `type`, `props`, and `children`:

```
React.createElement(type, props, children);
```

Let's take a look at each parameter in more detail.

The type parameter

The `type` parameter can be either a string or a `ReactClass`:

- A string could be an HTML tag name such as `'div'`, `'p'`, `'h1'`, and so on. React supports all the common HTML tags and attributes. For a complete list of HTML tags and attributes supported by React, you can refer to `http://facebook.github.io/react/docs/tags-and-attributes.html`.
- A `ReactClass` is created via the `React.createClass()` method. I'll introduce this in more detail in *Chapter 3, Create Your First React Component*.

The `type` parameter describes how an HTML tag or a `ReactClass` is going to be rendered. In our example, we're rendering the `h1` HTML tag.

The props parameter

The `props` parameter is a JavaScript object passed from a parent element to a child element (and not the other way around) with some properties that are considered immutable, that is, those that should not be changed.

While creating DOM elements with React, we can pass the `props` object with properties that represent the HTML attributes such as `class`, `style`, and so on. For example, run the following commands:

```
var React = require('react');
var ReactDOM = require('react-dom');
var reactElement = React.createElement('h1', { className: 'header' });
ReactDOM.render(reactElement, document.getElementById('react-
application'));
```

The preceding code will create an h1 HTML element with a class attribute set to header:

```
<h1 class="header" data-reactid=".0"></h1>
```

Notice that we name our property className rather than class. The reason is that the class keyword is reserved in JavaScript. If you use class as a property name, it will be ignored by React, and a helpful warning message will be printed on the web browser's console:

Warning: Unknown DOM property class. Did you mean className?

Use className instead.

You might be wondering what this data-reactid=".0" attribute is doing in our h1 tag? We didn't pass it to our props object, so where did it come from? It is added and used by React to track the DOM nodes; it might be removed in a future version of React.

The children parameter

The children parameter describes what child elements this element should have, if any. A child element can be any type of ReactNode: a virtual DOM element represented by a ReactElement, a string or a number represented by a ReactText, or an array of other ReactNodes, which is also called ReactFragment.

Let's take a look at this example:

```
var React = require('react');
var ReactDOM = require('react-dom');
var reactElement = React.createElement('h1', { className: 'header' },
'This is React');
ReactDOM.render(reactElement, document.getElementById('react-
application'));
```

The following code will create an h1 HTML element with a class attribute and a text node, This is React:

```
<h1 class="header" data-reactid=".0">This is React</h1>
```

The h1 tag is represented by a ReactElement, while the This is React string is represented by a ReactText.

Next, let's create a React element with a number of other React elements as it's children:

```
var React = require('react');
var ReactDOM = require('react-dom');

var h1 = React.createElement('h1', { className: 'header', key:
'header' }, 'This is React');
var p = React.createElement('p', { className: 'content', key:
'content' }, "And that's how it works.");
var reactFragment = [ h1, p ];
var section = React.createElement('section', { className: 'container'
}, reactFragment);

ReactDOM.render(section, document.getElementById('react-
application'));
```

We've created three React elements: h1, p, and section. h1 and p both have child text nodes, "This is React" and "And that's how it works.", respectively. The section has a child that is an array of two ReactElements, h1 and p, called reactFragment. This is also an array of ReactNodes. Each ReactElement in the reactFragment array must have a key property that helps React to identify that ReactElement. As a result, we get the following HTML markup:

```
<section class="container" data-reactid=".0">
  <h1 class="header" data-reactid=".0.$header">This is React</h1>
  <p class="content" data-reactid=".0.$content">And that's how it
works.</p>
</section>
```

Now we understand how to create React elements. What if we want to create a number of React elements of the same type? Does it mean that we need to call React.createElement('type') over and over again for each element of the same type? We can, but we don't need to because React provides us with a factory function called React.createFactory(). A factory function is a function that creates other functions. This is exactly what React.createFactory(type) does: it creates a function that produces a ReactElement of a given type.

Consider the following example:

```
var React = require('react');
var ReactDOM = require('react-dom');

var listItemElement1 = React.createElement('li', { className: 'item-
1', key: 'item-1' }, 'Item 1');
```

```
var listItemElement2 = React.createElement('li', { className: 'item-
2', key: 'item-2' }, 'Item 2');
var listItemElement3 = React.createElement('li', { className: 'item-
3', key: 'item-3' }, 'Item 3');

var reactFragment = [ listItemElement1, listItemElement2,
listItemElement3 ];
var listOfItems = React.createElement('ul', { className: 'list-of-
items' }, reactFragment);

ReactDOM.render(listOfItems, document.getElementById('react-
application'));
```

The preceding example produces this HTML:

```
<ul class="list-of-items" data-reactid=".0">
  <li class="item-1" data-reactid=".0.$item-1">Item 1</li>
  <li class="item-2" data-reactid=".0.$item-2">Item 2</li>
  <li class="item-3" data-reactid=".0.$item-3">Item 3</li>
</ul>
```

We can simplify it by first creating a factory function:

```
var React = require('react');
var ReactDOM = require('react-dom');

var createListItemElement = React.createFactory('li');

var listItemElement1 = createListItemElement({ className: 'item-1',
key: 'item-1' }, 'Item 1');
var listItemElement2 = createListItemElement({ className: 'item-2',
key: 'item-2' }, 'Item 2');
var listItemElement3 = createListItemElement({ className: 'item-3',
key: 'item-3' }, 'Item 3');

var reactFragment = [ listItemElement1, listItemElement2,
listItemElement3 ];
var listOfItems = React.createElement('ul', { className: 'list-of-
items' }, reactFragment);

ReactDOM.render(listOfItems, document.getElementById('react-
application'));
```

In the preceding example, we're first calling the `React.createFactory()` function and passing a `li` HTML tag name as a type parameter. Then, the `React.createFactory()` function returns a new function that we can use as a convenient shorthand to create elements of type `li`. We store a reference to this function in a variable called `createListItemElement`. Then, we call this function three times, and each time we only pass the `props` and `children` parameters, which are unique for each element. Notice that `React.createElement()` and `React.createFactory()` both expect the HTML tag name string (such as `li`) or the `ReactClass` object as a type parameter.

React provides us with a number of built-in factory functions to create the common HTML tags. You can call them from the `React.DOM` object; for example, `React.DOM.ul()`, `React.DOM.li()`, `React.DOM.div()`, and so on. Using them, we can simplify our previous example even further:

```
var React = require('react');
var ReactDOM = require('react-dom');

var listItemElement1 = React.DOM.li({ className: 'item-1', key: 'item-1' }, 'Item 1');
var listItemElement2 = React.DOM.li({ className: 'item-2', key: 'item-2' }, 'Item 2');
var listItemElement3 = React.DOM.li({ className: 'item-3', key: 'item-3' }, 'Item 3');

var reactFragment = [ listItemElement1, listItemElement2, listItemElement3 ];
var listOfItems = React.DOM.ul({ className: 'list-of-items' }, reactFragment);

ReactDOM.render(listOfItems, document.getElementById('react-application'));
```

Now we know how to create a tree of `ReactNode`s. However, there is one important line of code that we need to discuss before we can progress further:

```
ReactDOM.render(listOfItems, document.getElementById('react-application'));
```

As you might have already guessed, it renders our `ReactNode` tree to the DOM. Let's take a closer look at how it works.

Rendering React Elements

The `ReactDOM.render()` method takes three parameters: `ReactElement`, a regular `DOMElement`, and a callback function:

```
ReactDOM.render(ReactElement, DOMElement, callback);
```

`ReactElement` is a root element in the tree of `ReactNode`s that you've created. A regular `DOMElement` is a container DOM node for that tree. The `callback` is a function executed after the tree is rendered or updated. It's important to note that if this `ReactElement` was previously rendered to a parent DOM `Element`, then `ReactDOM.render()` will perform an update on the already rendered DOM tree and only mutate the DOM as it is necessary to reflect the latest version of the `ReactElement`. This is why a virtual DOM requires fewer DOM mutations.

So far, we've assumed that we're always creating our virtual DOM in a web browser. This is understandable because, after all, React is a user interface library, and all the user interfaces are rendered in a web browser. Can you think of a case when rendering a user interface on a client would be slow? Some of you might have already guessed that I am talking about the initial page load. The problem with the initial page load is the one I mentioned at the beginning of this chapter—we're not creating static web pages anymore. Instead, when a web browser loads our web application, it receives only the bare minimum HTML markup that is usually used as a container or a parent element for our web application. Then, our JavaScript code creates the rest of the DOM, but in order for it to do so it often needs to request extra data from the server. However, getting this data takes time. Once this data is received, our JavaScript code starts to mutate the DOM. We know that DOM mutations are slow. How can we solve this problem?

The solution is somewhat unexpected. Instead of mutating the DOM in a web browser, we mutate it on a server. Just like we would with our static web pages. A web browser will then receive an HTML that fully represents a user interface of our web application at the time of the initial page load. Sounds simple, but we can't mutate the DOM on a server because it doesn't exist outside a web browser. Or can we?

We have a virtual DOM that is just a JavaScript, and as you know using Node.js, we can run JavaScript on a server. So technically, we can use the React library on a server, and we can create our `ReactNode` tree on a server. The question is how can we render it to a string that we can send to a client?

React has a method called `ReactDOMServer.renderToString()` just to do this:

```
var ReactDOMServer = require('react-dom/server');
ReactDOMServer.renderToString(ReactElement);
```

It takes a `ReactElement` as a parameter and renders it to its initial HTML. Not only is this faster than mutating a DOM on a client, but it also improves the **Search Engine Optimization (SEO)** of your web application.

Speaking of generating static web pages, we can do this too with React:

```
var ReactDOMServer = require('react-dom/server');
ReactDOM.renderToStaticMarkup(ReactElement);
```

Similar to `ReactDOM.renderToString()`, this method also takes a `ReactElement` as a parameter and outputs an HTML string. However, it doesn't create the extra DOM attributes that React uses internally, it produces shorter HTML strings that we can transfer to the wire quickly.

Now you know not only how to create a virtual DOM tree using React elements, but you also know how to render it to a client and server. Our next question is whether we can do it quickly and in a more visual manner.

Creating React Elements with JSX

When we build our virtual DOM by constantly calling the `React.createElement()` method, it becomes quite hard to visually translate these multiple function calls into a hierarchy of HTML tags. Don't forget that, even though we're working with a virtual DOM, we're still creating a structure layout for our content and user interface. Wouldn't it be great to be able to visualize that layout easily by simply looking at our React code?

JSX is an optional HTML-like syntax that allows us to create a virtual DOM tree without using the `React.createElement()` method.

Let's take a look at the previous example that we created without JSX:

```
var React = require('react');
var ReactDOM = require('react-dom');

var listItemElement1 = React.DOM.li({ className: 'item-1', key: 'item-
1' }, 'Item 1');
var listItemElement2 = React.DOM.li({ className: 'item-2', key: 'item-
2' }, 'Item 2');
```

```
var listItemElement3 = React.DOM.li({ className: 'item-3', key: 'item-
3' }, 'Item 3');

var reactFragment = [ listItemElement1, listItemElement2,
listItemElement3 ];
var listOfItems = React.DOM.ul({ className: 'list-of-items' },
reactFragment);

ReactDOM.render(listOfItems, document.getElementById('react-
application'));
```

Translate this to the one with JSX:

```
var React = require('react');
var ReactDOM = require('react-dom');

var listOfItems = <ul className="list-of-items">
                      <li className="item-1">Item 1</li>
                      <li className="item-2">Item 2</li>
                      <li className="item-3">Item 3</li>
                  </ul>;

ReactDOM.render(listOfItems, document.getElementById('react-
application'));
```

As you can see, JSX allows us to write HTML-like syntax in our JavaScript code. More importantly, we can now clearly see what our HTML layout will look like once it's rendered. JSX is a convenience tool and it comes with a price in the form of an additional transformation step. Transformation of the JSX syntax into valid JavaScript syntax must happen before our "invalid" JavaScript code is interpreted.

In our previous chapter, we installed the `babely` module that transforms our JSX syntax into a JavaScript one. This transformation happens every time we run our `default` task from `gulpfile.js`:

```
gulp.task('default', function () {
  return browserify('./source/app.js')
        .transform(babelify)
        .bundle()
        .pipe(source('snapterest.js'))
        .pipe(gulp.dest('./build/'));
});
```

As you can see, the `.transform(babelify)` function call transforms JSX into JavaScript before bundling it with the other JavaScript code.

To test our transformation, run this command:

```
gulp
```

Then, navigate to the `~/snapterest/build/` directory, and open `index.html` in a web browser. You will see a list of three items.

The React team has built an online JSX Compiler that you can use to test your understanding of how JSX works at `http://facebook.github.io/react/jsx-compiler.html`.

Using JSX, you might feel very unusual in the beginning, but it can become a very intuitive and convenient tool to use. The best part is that you can choose whether to use it or not. I found that JSX saves me development time, so I chose to use it in this project that we're building, and in the code samples I will be sharing with you in this book. If you choose to not use it, then I believe that you have learned enough in this chapter to be able to translate the JSX syntax into a JavaScript code with the `React.createElement()` function calls.

If you have a question about what we have discussed in this chapter, then you can refer to `https://github.com/fedosejev/react-essentials` and create a new issue.

Summary

We started this chapter by discussing the issues with single web page applications and how they can be addressed. Then, we learned what a virtual DOM is and how React allows us to build it. We also installed React and created our first React element using only JavaScript. Then, we also learned how to render React elements in a web browser and on a server. Finally, we looked at a simpler way of creating React elements with JSX.

In the next chapter, we'll dive deeper into the world of React components.

3
Create Your First React Component

In the previous chapter, we learned how to create React elements and how to use them to render the HTML markup. You've seen how easy it is to produce React elements using JSX. At this point, you know enough about React in order to create the static web pages that we discussed in *Chapter 2, Create Your First React Element*. However, I bet that's not the reason why you've decided to learn React. You don't want to just build websites made of static HTML elements. You want to build interactive user interfaces that react to user and server events. What does it mean to react to an event? How can a static HTML element *react*? How can a React element react? In this chapter, we'll answer these questions and many other questions while introducing ourselves to React components.

Stateless versus stateful

To react means to switch from one state to another. This means that you need to have a state in the first place and the ability to change that state. Have we mentioned a state or the ability to change that state in React elements? No. They are stateless. Their sole purpose is to construct and render virtual DOM elements. In fact, we want them to render in the exact same way, given that we provide them the exact same set of parameters. We want them to be consistent because it makes it easy for us to reason about them. That's one of the key benefits of using the React library—the ease of reasoning how our web application works.

How can we add a state to our stateless React elements? If we can't encapsulate a state in React elements, then we should encapsulate React elements in something that already has a state. Think of a simple state machine that represents a user interface. Every user action triggers a change of a state in that state machine. Every state is represented by a different React element. In the React library, this state machine is called a React Component.

Creating your first stateless React component

Let's take a look at the following example of how to create a React component:

```
var React = require('react');
var ReactDOM = require('react-dom');

var ReactClass = React.createClass({
  render: function () {
    return React.createElement('h1', { className: 'header' }, 'React
Component');
  }
});
var reactComponentElement = React.createElement(ReactClass);
var reactComponent = ReactDOM.render(reactComponentElement, document.
getElementById('react-application'));
```

Some of the preceding code should already look familiar to you, and the rest can be broken down into three simple steps:

1. Creating a React class.

2. Creating a React component element.

3. Creating a React component.

Let's take a closer look at how we can create a React component:

1. Create a `ReactClass` by calling the `React.createClass()` function and providing a specification object as its parameter. In this chapter, we'll focus on learning about the specification objects in more detail.

2. Create a `ReactComponentElement` by calling the `React.createElement()` function and providing our `ReactClass` as its `type` parameter. In *Chapter 2, Create Your First React Element*, we learned that the `type` parameter can be either a string or a `ReactClass`. In this chapter, you'll learn more about the latter one.

3. Create a `ReactComponent` by calling the `ReactDOM.render()` function and providing our `ReactComponentElement` as its `element` parameter.

The **specification object** that you pass as a parameter to `React.createClass()` is where your component's look and feel is defined. Specification is the definition of your React component. From now on, in this chapter, we'll refer to a specification object as a React component, and in the rest of the chapter we will learn about this very important concept.

The specification object encapsulates a component's state and describes how a component is rendered. At the very minimum, the React component needs to have a `render()` method so that it returns at least `null` or `false`. Here is an example of a specification object in its simplest form:

```
{
  render: function () {
    return null;
  }
}
```

As you can guess, the `render()` function is responsible for telling React how to render your React component. It can return `null`, as in the preceding example, and nothing will be rendered. Or it can return a `ReactElement` that we learned how to create in *Chapter 2*, *Create Your First React Element*:

```
{
  render: function () {
    return React.createElement('h1', { className: 'header' }, 'React
Component');
  }
}
```

This example shows how we can encapsulate our React element inside our React component. We create a `ReactElement` of type `h1` with the properties object and a `ReactText` as its only child. Then, we return it when the `render()` method of our React component is called. The fact that we encapsulated our React element inside a React component doesn't affect how it will be rendered:

```
<h1 class="header" data-reactid=".0">React Component</h1>
```

As you can see, the produced HTML markup is identical to the one we created in *Chapter 2*, *Create Your First React Element*, without using the React component. In this case, you might be wondering what's the benefit of having a `render()` function if we can render the exact same markup without it?

The advantage of having a `render()` function is that, as with any other function, before it returns a value, it can choose what value to return. So far, you've seen two examples of the `render()` function: one that returns `null` and one that returns a React element. We can merge the two and add a condition that decides what to render:

```
{
  render: function () {
    var elementState = {
      isHidden: true
```

```
  };

  if (elementState.isHidden) {
    return null;
  }

  return React.createElement('h1', { className: 'header' }, 'React
Component');
  }
}
```

In this example, we created the `elementState` variable that references an object with a single `isHidden` property. This object acts as a state for our React element. If we want to hide our React element, then we need to set the value of `elementState.isHidden` to `true`, and our `render` function will return `null`. In this case, React will render nothing. Logically, by setting `elementState.isHidden` to `false`, will return our React element and the expected HTML markup will be rendered. The question you might ask is: how do we set the value of `elementState.isHidden` to `false`? Or to `true`? Or how do we change it in general?

Let's think of scenarios in which we might want to change that state. One of them is when a user interacts with our user interface. Another one is when a server sends data. Or when a certain amount of time passes and then we want to render something else. Our `render()` function is not aware of all these events and it shouldn't be because its sole purpose is to return a React element based on the data that we pass to it. How do we pass data to it?

There are two ways to pass data to a `render()` function using the React API:

- `this.props`
- `this.state`

`this.props` should look familiar to you. In *Chapter 2, Create Your First React Element,* we learned that the `React.createElement()` function accepts the `props` parameter. We used it to pass attributes to our HTML elements, but we didn't discuss what happens behind the scene and why attributes passed to the `props` object get rendered.

Any data that you put in the `props` object and pass to the `React.createElement()` function can be accessed inside the `render()` function of `ReactComponent` via `this.props`. Once you have accessed data from `this.props`, you can render it:

```
{
  render: function () {
    var elementState = {
```

```
      isHidden: true
    };

    if (elementState.isHidden) {
      return null;
    }

    return React.createElement('h1', { className: 'header' }, this.
props.header);
    }
  }
```

In this example, we're using this.props inside our render() function to access the header property. We're then passing this.props.header directly to the React.createElement() function as a child string element.

In the preceding example, we can pass the value of isHidden as another property of the this.props object:

```
{
  render: function () {
    if (this.props.isHidden) {
      return null;
    }

    return React.createElement('h1', { className: 'header' }, this.
props.header);
  }
}
```

We can also use this.props to compute data that needs to be rendered:

```
{
  render: function () {
    if (this.props.isHidden) {
      return null;
    }

    var header = this.props.tweets.length + ' Latest Tweets';
    return React.createElement('h1', { className: 'header' }, header);
  }
}
```

As you can see, we're accessing an array of tweets via `this.props.tweets` and getting its `length` property. Then, we're concatenating a string `' Latest Tweets'` to it. The resulting string is stored in a `header` variable, and this is our computed child string element that we're passing to the `React.createElement()` function.

Notice that in our previous example, instead of storing `isHidden` in a `render()` function, we're passing it via `this.props`. We removed our `elementState` object from it because we don't need to worry about the state in our `render()` function. It's a pure function, which means that it shouldn't mutate the state or access the real DOM, or otherwise interact with a web browser. Remember that we might want to use React on a server, where we have no web browser, and we should expect the `render()` function to produce the same result regardless of the environment.

If our `render()` function doesn't manage the state, then how do we manage it? How do we set the state, and how do we update it while handling user or browser events in React?

Earlier in this chapter, we learned that in React we can represent a user interface with React components. There are two types of React components:

- With a state
- Without a state

Hold on, didn't we say that React components are state machines? Surely, every state machine needs to have a state. You're correct; however, it's a good practice to keep as many React components stateless as possible.

React components are composable. As a result, we can have a hierarchy of React components. Imagine that we have a parent React component that has two child components, and each of them in turn has another two child components. All the components are stateful and they can manage their own state:

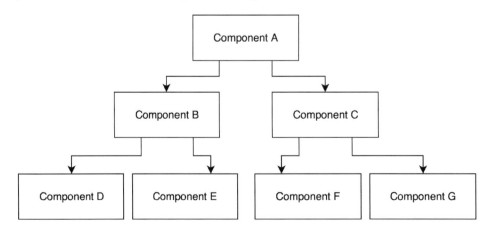

How easy will it be to figure out what the last child component in the hierarchy will render if the top component in the hierarchy updates its state? Not easy. There is a design pattern that removes this unnecessary complexity. The idea is to separate your components into two concerns: how to handle the user interface interaction logic and how to render data.

- The minority of your React components are stateful. They should be at the top of your components' hierarchy. They encapsulate all of the interaction logic, manage the user interface state, and pass that state down the hierarchy to stateless components, using `props`.

- The majority of your React components are stateless. They receive the state data from their parent components via `this.props` and render that data accordingly.

In our previous example, we received the `isHidden` state data via `this.props` and then we rendered that data. Our component was stateless.

Next, let's create our first stateful component.

Creating your first stateful React component

Stateful components are the most appropriate place for your application to handle the interaction logic and manage the state. They make it easier for you to reason out how your application works. This reasoning plays a key role in building maintainable web applications.

React stores the component's state in `this.state`, and it sets the initial value of `this.state` to the value returned by the `getInitialState()` function. However, it's up to us to tell React what the `getInitialState()` function will return. Let's add this function to our React component:

```
{
  getInitialState: function () {
    return {
      isHidden: false
    };
  },

  render: function () {
    if (this.state.isHidden) {
```

```
        return null;
    }

    return React.createElement('h1', { className: 'header' }, 'React
Component');
    }
}
```

In this example, our `getInitialState()` function returns an object with a single `isHidden` property that is set to `false`. This is the initial state of our React component and our user interface. Notice that in our `render()` function, we're now referring to `this.state.isHidden` instead of `this.props.isHidden`.

Earlier in this chapter, you learned that we can pass data to the component's `render()` function via `this.props` or `this.state`. So, what is the difference between the two?

- `this.props` stores read-only data that is passed from the parent. It belongs to the parent and cannot be changed by its children. This data should be considered immutable.

- `this.state` stores data that is private to the component. It can be changed by the component. The component will rerender itself when the state is updated.

How do we update a component's state? There is a common way of informing React of a state change using `setState(data, callback)`. This function takes two parameters:

- The `data` function that represents the next state

- The `callback` function, which you will rarely need to use because React keeps your user interface up to date for you

How does React keep your user interface up to date? It calls the component's `render()` function every time you update the component's state, including any child components which are rerendered as well. In fact, it rerenders the entire virtual DOM every time our `render()` function is called.

When you call the `this.setState()` function and pass it a data object that represents the next state, React will merge that next state with the current state. During the merge, React will overwrite the current state with the next state. The current state that is not overwritten by the next state will become part of the next state.

Imagine that this is our current state:

```
{
    isHidden: true,
    title: 'Stateful React Component'
}
```

We call `this.setState(nextState)` where `nextState` is as follows:

```
{
    isHidden: false
}
```

React will merge the two states into a new one:

```
{
    isHidden: false,
    title: 'Stateful React Component'
}
```

The `isHidden` property is updated and the `title` property is not deleted or updated in any way.

Now that we know how to update our component's state, let's create a stateful component that reacts to a user event:

```
{
    getInitialState: function () {
        return {
            isHeaderHidden: false,
            title: 'Stateful React Component'
        };
    },

    handleClick: function () {
        this.setState({
            isHeaderHidden: !this.state.isHeaderHidden
        });
    },

    render: function () {
        var headerElement = React.createElement('h1', { className:
'header', key: 'header' }, this.state.title);
        var buttonElement = React.createElement('button', { className:
'btn btn-default', onClick: this.handleClick, key: 'button' }, 'Toggle
header');
```

```
    if (this.state.isHeaderHidden) {
      return React.createElement('div', null, [ buttonElement ]);
    }

    return React.createElement('div', null, [ buttonElement,
  headerElement ]);
    }
  }
```

In this example, we're creating a toggle button that shows and hides a header. The first thing we do is set our initial state object by returning it to the getInitialState() function. Our initial state has two properties: isHeaderHidden that is set to false and title that is set to 'Stateful React Component'. Now we can access this state object in our render() function via this.state. Inside our render() function, we create three React elements: h1, button, and div. Our div element acts as a parent element for our h1 and button elements. However, in one case we create our div element with two children, headerElement and buttonElement, and in the other case we create it with only one child, buttonElement. The case we choose depends on the value of this.state. isHeaderHidden. The current state of our component directly affects what the render() function will render. While this should look familiar to you, there is something new in this example that we haven't seen before.

Notice that we introduced a new property on our ReactComponent object, called handleClick(), which is a function that has no special meaning to React. It's part of our application logic, and we use it to handle the onClick events. You can add your own properties to the ReactComponent object. All of these will be available via a this reference, which you can access from any other function that itself is a property of the component object. For example, we are accessing a state object via this.state in both the render() and handleClick() functions.

What does our handleClick() function do? It updates our component's state by setting the new value of the isHeaderHidden property to the opposite of the existing one that it accesses via this.state.isHeaderHidden:

```
this.setState({
  isHeaderHidden: !this.state.isHeaderHidden
});
```

Our handleClick() function reacts to a user interaction with our user interface. Our user interface is a button element that a user can click on, and we can attach an event handler to it. In React, you can attach event handlers to a React element by passing them to the props parameter in the createElement() function:

```
React.createElement('button', { className: 'btn btn-default', onClick:
this.handleClick }, 'Toggle header');
```

React uses the **CamelCase** naming convention for event handlers; for example, onClick. You can find a list of all the supported events at http://facebook. github.io/react/docs/events.html#supported-events.

By default, React triggers the event handlers in the bubble phase, but you can tell React to trigger them in the capture phase by appending Capture to the event name; for example, onClickCapture.

React wraps a browser's native events into the SyntheticEvent object to ensure that all the supported events behave identically in Internet Explorer 8 and above.

The SyntheticEvent object provides the same API as the native browser's event, which means that you can use the stopPropagation() and preventDefault() methods as usual. If for some reason, you need to access that native browser's event, then you can do this via the nativeEvent property. To enable touch-event handling, simply call React.initializeTouchEvents(true).

Notice that passing the onClick property to our createElement() function in the previous example does not create an inline event handler in the rendered HTML markup:

```
<button class="btn btn-default" data-reactid=".0.$button">Toggle
header</button>
```

This is because React doesn't actually attach event handlers to the DOM nodes themselves. Instead, React listens for all the events at the top level using a single event listener, and delegates them to their appropriate event handlers.

In the previous example, you learned how to create a stateful React component that a user can interact with and change its state. We created and attached an event handler to the click event that updates the value of the isHeaderHidden property. But have you noticed that the user interaction does not update the value of another property that we store in our state, title? Does that seem odd to you? We have data in our state that doesn't ever get changed. This observation raises an important question; what should we *not* put in our state?

Ask yourself a question: what data can I remove from a component's state and still keep its user interface always up to date? Keep asking and keep removing that data until you're absolutely certain that there is nothing left to remove without breaking your user interface.

In our example, we have the `title` property in our state object that we can move to our `render()` function without breaking the interactivity of our toggle button. The component will still work as expected:

```
{
  getInitialState: function () {
    return {
      isHeaderHidden: false
    };
  },

  handleClick: function () {
    this.setState({
      isHeaderHidden: !this.state.isHeaderHidden
    });
  },

  render: function () {
    var title = 'Stateful React Component';

    var headerElement = React.createElement('h1', { className:
'header', key: 'header' }, title);
    var buttonElement = React.createElement('button', { className:
'btn btn-default', onClick: this.handleClick, key: 'button' }, 'Toggle
header');

    if (this.state.isHeaderHidden) {
      return React.createElement('div', null, [ buttonElement ]);
    }

    return React.createElement('div', null, [ buttonElement,
headerElement ]);
  }
}
```

On the other hand, if we move the `isHeaderHidden` property out of a state object, then we'll break the interactivity of our component because our `render()` function will not be triggered automatically by React every time a user clicks on our button. This is an example of broken interactivity:

```
{
  getInitialState: function () {
    return {};
  },
```

```
  isHeaderHidden: false,

  handleClick: function () {
    this.isHeaderHidden = !this.isHeaderHidden;
  },

  render: function () {
    var title = 'Stateful React Component';

    var headerElement = React.createElement('h1', { className:
'header', key: 'header' }, title);
    var buttonElement = React.createElement('button', { className:
'btn btn-default', onClick: this.handleClick, key: 'button' }, 'Toggle
header');

    if (this.state.isHeaderHidden) {
      return React.createElement('div', null, [ buttonElement ]);
    }

    return React.createElement('div', null, [ buttonElement,
headerElement ]);
  }
}
```

This is an anti-pattern.

Remember this rule of thumb: a component's state should store data that a component's event handlers may change over time in order to rerender a component's user interface and keep it up to date. Keep the minimal possible representation of a component's state in a `state` object, and compute the rest of the data based on what's in `state` and `props` inside a component's `render()` function. Anything that you put in `state`, you'll need to update yourself. Anything that you put in `render()` will automatically get updated by React. Take advantage of React.

Summary

In this chapter, we reached an important milestone: we learned how to encapsulate a state and create interactive user interfaces by creating React components. We discussed stateless and stateful React components, and the difference between them. We talked about the browser events and how to handle them in React.

In the next chapter, we'll be planning our Snapterest web application. You'll learn how to solve a problem with React and how to create composable React components.

4
Make Your React Components Reactive

Now that you know how to create React components with and without a state, we can start composing React components together and build more complex user interfaces. In fact, it's time for us to start building our web application, called **Snapterest**, that we discussed in *Chapter 1, Installing Powerful Tools for Your Project*. While doing this, we'll learn how to plan your React application and create composable React components. Let's begin.

Solving a problem using React

Before you start writing code for your web application, you need to think about the problems that your web application is going to solve. It's very important to understand that defining the problem as clearly and as early as possible is the most important step toward a successful solution—a useful web application. If you fail to define your problem early in your development process, or you define it inaccurately, then later on you'll have to stop, rethink about what you're doing, throw away a piece of the code that you have already written, and write a new one. This is a wasteful approach, and as a professional software developer your time is very valuable, not only to you but also to your organization, so it's in your best interests to invest it wisely. Earlier in this book, I stressed on the fact that one of the benefits of using React is code reuse, which means that you'll be able to do more in less time. However, before we take a look at the React code, let's first discuss the problem, keeping React in mind.

We'll be building Snapterest—a web application that receives tweets from a Snapkite Engine server in a real-time manner and displays them one at a time to a user. We don't actually know when Snapterest will receive a new tweet, but when it does, it will display that new tweet for at least 1.5 seconds so that the user has enough time to take a look at it and click on it. Clicking on a tweet will add it to an existing collection of tweets or create a new one. Finally, users will be able to export their collection to an HTML markup code.

This is a very high-level description of what we're going to build. Let's break it down into a list of smaller tasks:

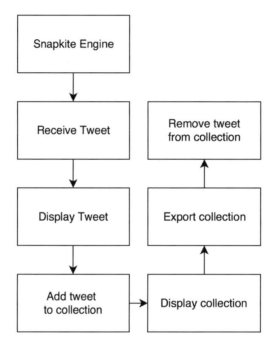

1. Receive tweets from the Snapkite Engine server in real time.
2. Display one tweet at a time for at least 1.5 seconds.
3. Add tweets to a collection on a user click event.
4. Display a list of tweets in a collection.
5. Create an HTML markup code for a collection and export it.
6. Remove tweets from a collection on a user click event.

Can you identify which tasks can be solved using React? Remember that React is a user interface library, so anything that describes the user interface and interactions with that user interface can be addressed with React. In the preceding list, React can take care of all the tasks except for the first one because it describes data fetching and not the user interface in any way. Task 1 will be solved with another library that we'll discuss in the next chapter. Tasks 2 and 4 describe something that needs to be displayed. They are perfect candidates for React components. Tasks 3 and 6 describe the user events, and as we've seen in *Chapter 3, Create Your First React Component*, user events handling can be encapsulated in React components as well. Can you think of how task 5 can be solved with React? Remember in *Chapter 2, Create Your First React Element*, we discussed the `ReactDOMServer.renderToStaticMarkup()` method that renders the React element to a static HTML markup string. That's exactly what we need in order to solve task 5.

Now that we've identified a potential solution for each individual task, let's think about how are we going to put them together and create a fully functional web application.

There are two ways to build composable React applications:

- You can start by building individual React components and then compose them together into higher-level React components, moving up the component hierarchy.
- You can start from the topmost React element and then implement its child components, moving down the component hierarchy.

The second strategy has the advantage of seeing and understanding the big picture of your application's architecture. I think it's important to understand how everything fits together before we can think of how individual pieces of functionality are implemented.

Planning your React application

There are two simple guidelines we need to follow when planning your React application:

- Each React component should represent a single user interface element in your web application. It should encapsulate the smallest element possible that can potentially be reused.

- Multiple React components should be composed into a single React component. Ultimately, your entire user interface should be encapsulated in one React component.

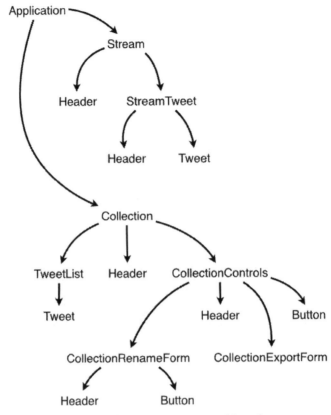

Diagram of our React components hierarchy

We'll begin with our topmost React component, Application. It will encapsulate our entire React application, and it will have two child components: the Stream and Collection components. The Stream component will be responsible for connecting to a stream of tweets, and receiving and displaying the latest tweet. The Stream component will have two child components: StreamTweet and Header. The StreamTweet component will be responsible for displaying the latest tweet. It will be composed of the Header and Tweet components. A Header component will render a header. It will have no child components. A Tweet component will render an image from a tweet. Notice how we're planning to reuse the Header component twice already.

The `Collection` component will be responsible for displaying the collection controls and a list of tweets. It will have two child components: `CollectionControls` and `TweetList`. The `CollectionControls` will have two child components: the `CollectionRenameForm` component that will render a form to rename a collection, and the `CollectionExportForm` component that will render a form to export a collection to a service called **CodePen**, which is an HTML, CSS, and JavaScript playground website. You can learn more about CodePen at `http://codepen.io`. As you might have noticed, we'll reuse the `Header` and `Button` components in the `CollectionRenameForm` and `CollectionControls` components. Our `TweetList` component will render a list of tweets. Each tweet will be rendered by a `Tweet` component. We'll be reusing the `Header` component once again in our `Collection` component. In fact, in total, we'll be reusing the `Header` component five times. That's a win for us. As we discussed in the previous chapter, we should keep as many React components stateless as possible. So only 5 out of 11 components will store the state, which are:

- `Application`
- `CollectionControls`
- `CollectionRenameForm`
- `Stream`
- `StreamTweet`

Now that we have a plan, we can start implementing it.

Creating a container React component

Let's start by editing our application's main JavaScript file. Replace the contents of the `~/snapterest/source/app.js` file with the following code snippet:

```
var React = require('react');
var ReactDOM = require('react-dom');
var Application = require('./components/Application.react');

ReactDOM.render(<Application />, document.getElementById('react-
application'));
```

There are only four lines of code in this file, and as you can guess, they provide `document.getElementById('react-application')` as a deployment target for the `<Application />` component and render `<Application />` to the DOM. The whole user interface for our web application will be encapsulated in one React component, `Application`.

Next, navigate to `~/snapterest/source/components/` and create the `Application.react.js` file inside this directory. All of our React components will have their filenames ending with `react.js`. This convention allows us to easily distinguish between React and non-React source JavaScript files.

Let's take a look at the contents of the `Application.react.js` file:

```
var React = require('react');
var Stream = require('./Stream.react');
var Collection = require('./Collection.react');

var Application = React.createClass({

  getInitialState: function () {
    return {
      collectionTweets: {}
    };
  },

  addTweetToCollection: function (tweet) {
    var collectionTweets = this.state.collectionTweets;

    collectionTweets[tweet.id] = tweet;

    this.setState({
      collectionTweets: collectionTweets
    });
  },

  removeTweetFromCollection: function (tweet) {
    var collectionTweets = this.state.collectionTweets;

    delete collectionTweets[tweet.id];

    this.setState({
      collectionTweets: collectionTweets
    });
  },

  removeAllTweetsFromCollection: function () {
    this.setState({
      collectionTweets: {}
    });
  },

  render: function () {
    return (
      <div className="container-fluid">
```

```
            <div className="row">
              <div className="col-md-4 text-center">

                <Stream onAddTweetToCollection={this.addTweetToCollection}
/>

              </div>
              <div className="col-md-8">

                <Collection
                  tweets={this.state.collectionTweets}
                  onRemoveTweetFromCollection={this.
removeTweetFromCollection}
                  onRemoveAllTweetsFromCollection={this.
removeAllTweetsFromCollection} />

              </div>
            </div>

          </div>
        );
      }
    });

    module.exports = Application;
```

This component has significantly more code than our app.js file, but this code can be easily divided into three logical parts:

- Importing dependency modules
- Defining React components
- Exporting a React component as a module

You will see this logical separation in most of our React components because they are wrapped into the **CommonJS** module pattern that allows us to easily require them with Browserify. In fact, the first and the third parts of this source file are related to how CommonJS works and have nothing to do with how React works. The purpose of using this module pattern is to break our application into modules that can be easily reused. Because the React component and CommonJS module pattern both encapsulate the code and make it portable, they naturally work great together. So, we end up encapsulating our user interface logic in a React component and then encapsulate that React component in the CommonJS module. It then can be used in any other module that wants to reuse this encapsulated React component.

In our first logical part of the Application.react.js file, we're importing the dependency modules using the require() function:

```
var React = require('react');
var Stream = require('./Stream.react');
var Collection = require('./Collection.react');
```

Our Application component will have two child components that we need to import:

- The Stream component will render a stream section of our user interface
- The Collection component will render a collection section of our user interface

We also need to import the React library as another module. Notice that this code is still part of the CommonJS module pattern, not React.

The second logical part of the Application.react.js file creates the React Application component with the following methods:

- getInitialState()
- addTweetToCollection()
- removeTweetFromCollection()
- removeAllTweetsFromCollection()
- render()

Only the getInitialState() and render() methods are part of the React API. All the other methods are part of our application logic that this component encapsulates. We'll take a closer look at each of them right after we discuss what this component renders inside its render() function:

```
render: function () {
  return (
    <div className="container-fluid">

      <div className="row">
        <div className="col-md-4 text-center">

          <Stream onAddTweetToCollection={this.addTweetToCollection}
/>

        </div>
        <div className="col-md-8">
```

```
        <Collection
          tweets={this.state.collectionTweets}
         onRemoveTweetFromCollection={this.
removeTweetFromCollection}
       onRemoveAllTweetsFromCollection={this.
removeAllTweetsFromCollection} />

        </div>
      </div>

    </div>
  );
}
```

As you can see, it defines the layout of our web page using the Bootstrap framework. If you're not familiar with Bootstrap, I strongly recommend that you visit http://getbootstrap.com and read the documentation. Learning this framework will empower you to prototype user interfaces in a fast and easy way. Even if you don't know Bootstrap, it's quite easy to understand what's going on. We're dividing our web page into two columns: a smaller one and a larger one. The smaller one contains our Stream React component and the larger one contains our Collection component. You can imagine that our web page is divided into two unequal parts and both of them contain the React components.

This is how we're using our Stream component:

```
<Stream onAddTweetToCollection={this.addTweetToCollection} />
```

The Stream component has an onAddTweetToCollection property, and our Application component passes its own addTweetToCollection() function as a value for this property. addTweetToCollection() adds a tweet to a collection. It's one of the custom methods that we define in our Application component, and we can refer to it using this keyword.

Let's take a look at what the addTweetToCollection() function does:

```
addTweetToCollection: function (tweet) {
  var collectionTweets = this.state.collectionTweets;

  collectionTweets[tweet.id] = tweet;

  this.setState({
    collectionTweets: collectionTweets
  });
},
```

This function references `CollectionTweets` that are stored in the current state, adds a new tweet to a `collectionTweets` object, and updates the state by calling the `setState()` function. A new tweet is passed as an argument when the `addTweetToCollection()` function is called inside a `Stream` component. This is an example of how a child component can update its parent component's state.

This an important mechanism in React and it works as follows:

1. A parent component passes a callback function as a property to its child component. A child component can access this callback function via the `this.props` variable.

2. Whenever a child component wants to update the parent component's state, it calls that callback function and passes all the necessary data to a new parent component's state.

3. A parent component updates its state, and as you already know, this state updates and triggers the `render()` function that re-renders all the child components, as necessary.

This is how a child component interacts with a parent component. This interaction allows a child component to delegate the application's state management to its parent component, and it is only concerned with how to render itself. Now, when you've learned this pattern, you will be using it again and again because most of your React components should stay stateless. Only a few parent components should store and manage your application's state. This best practice allows us to logically group React components by the two different concerns that they address:

- Manage the application's state and render

- Only render and delegate the application's state management to a parent component

Our `Application` component has a second child component, `Collection`:

```
<Collection
  tweets={this.state.collectionTweets}
  onRemoveTweetFromCollection={this.removeTweetFromCollection}
onRemoveAllTweetsFromCollection={this.removeAllTweetsFromCollection}
  />
```

This component has a number of properties:

- `tweets`: This refers to our current collection of tweets
- `onRemoveTweetFromCollection`: This refers to a function that removes a particular tweet from our collection
- `onRemoveAllTweetsFromCollection`: This refers to a function that removes all the tweets from our collection

You can see that the `Collection` component's properties are only concerned about how to:

- Access the application's state
- Mutate the application's state

As you can guess, the `onRemoveTweetFromCollection` and `onRemoveAllTweetsFromCollection` functions allow the `Collection` component to mutate the `Application` component's state. On the other hand, the `tweets` property propagates the `Application` component's state to the `Collection` component so that it can gain a read-only access to that state.

Can you recognize the single direction of data flow between the `Application` and `Collection` components? Here's how it works:

1. The `collectionTweets` data is initialized in the `Application` component's `getInitialState()` method.
2. The `collectionTweets` data is passed to the `Collection` component as the `tweets` property.
3. The `Collection` component calls the `removeTweetFromCollection` and `removeAllTweetsFromCollection` functions that update the `collectionTweets` data in the `Application` component, and the cycle starts again.

Notice that the `Collection` component cannot directly mutate the `Application` component's state. The `Collection` component has read-only access to that state via `this.props` object, and the only way to update the parent component's state is to call the callback functions that are passed by the parent component. In the `Collection` component, these callback functions are `this.props.onRemoveTweetFromCollection` and `this.props.onRemoveAllTweetsFromCollection`.

This simple mental model of how data flows in our React component hierarchy will help us increase the number of components we use, without increasing the complexity of how our user interface works. For example, it can have 10 levels of nested React components, as follows:

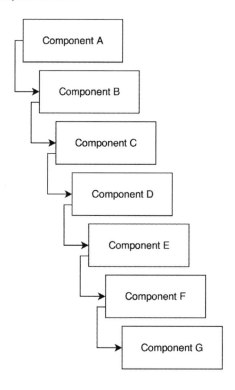

If Component G wants to mutate the state of root Component A, it would do it in the exact same way that Component B, or Component F, or any other component in this hierarchy would. However, in React, you shouldn't pass data from Component A directly to Component G. Instead, you should first pass it to Component B, then to Component C, then to Component D, and so on until you finally reach Component G. Component B to Component F will have to carry some "transit" properties that are actually only meant for Component G. This might look like a waste of time, but this design makes it easy for us to debug our application and be able to reason out how it works. There are always strategies to optimize your application's architecture. One of them is to use **Flux**, which we'll discuss later in this book.

Before we finish discussing our `Application` component, let's take a look at the two methods that mutate its state:

```
removeTweetFromCollection: function (tweet) {
  var collectionTweets = this.state.collectionTweets;

  delete collectionTweets[tweet.id];

  this.setState({
    collectionTweets: collectionTweets
  });
},
```

The `removeTweetFromCollection()` method removes a tweet from a collection of tweets that we store in the `Application` component's state. It takes the current `collectionTweets` object from the component's state, deletes a tweet with a given ID from that object, and updates the component's state with an updated `collectionTweets` object.

On the other hand, the `removeAllTweetsFromCollection()` method removes all the tweets from the component's state:

```
removeAllTweetsFromCollection: function () {
  this.setState({
    collectionTweets: {}
  });
},
```

Both of these methods are called from a child's `Collection` component because that component has no other way to mutate the `Application` component's state.

Summary

In this chapter, we learned how to solve a problem with React. We started by breaking down the problem into smaller individual problems and then discussed how we can address them using React. Then, we created a list of React components that we needed to implement. Finally, we created our first composable React component and learned how a parent component interacts with its child components. In the next chapter, we'll implement our child components and learn about React's lifecycle methods.

5
Use Your React Components with Another Library

React is a great library used for building user interfaces. What if we want to integrate it with another library that is responsible for receiving data? In the previous chapter, we outlined five tasks that our Snapterest web application should be able to perform. We decided that four of them were related to the user interface, but one of them was all about receiving data; receive tweets from the Snapkite Engine server in real time.

In this chapter, we'll learn how to integrate React with the external JavaScript library and what React component lifecycle methods are, all while solving the very important task of receiving data.

Using another library in your React component

As we discussed earlier in this book, our Snapterest web application will consume a live stream of tweets. In *Chapter 1, Installing Powerful Tools for Your Project*, you installed the **Snapkite Engine** library that connects to the Twitter Streaming API, filters the incoming tweets, and sends them to our client application. In turn, our client application needs a way of connecting to that live stream and listening for the new tweets.

Luckily, we don't need to implement this functionality ourselves because we can reuse another Snapkite module called `snapkite-stream-client`. Let's install this module.

Navigate to the ~/snapterest directory and run the following command:

npm install --save snapkite-stream-client

It will install the snapkite-stream-client module, and add it to package.json as a dependency.

Now we're ready to reuse the snapkite-stream-client module in one of our React components.

In the previous chapter, we created the Application component with two child components: Stream and Collection. In this chapter, we'll create our Stream component.

Let's start by creating the ~/snapterest/source/components/Stream.react.js file:

```
var React = require('react');
var SnapkiteStreamClient = require('snapkite-stream-client');
var StreamTweet = require('./StreamTweet.react');
var Header = require('./Header.react');

var Stream = React.createClass({

  getInitialState: function () {
    return {
      tweet: null
    }
  },

  componentDidMount: function () {
    SnapkiteStreamClient.initializeStream(this.handleNewTweet);
  },

  componentWillUnmount: function () {
    SnapkiteStreamClient.destroyStream();
  },

  handleNewTweet: function (tweet) {
    this.setState({
      tweet: tweet
    });
  },

  render: function () {
```

```
      var tweet = this.state.tweet;

      if (tweet) {
        return (
          <StreamTweet
          tweet={tweet}
          onAddTweetToCollection={this.props.onAddTweetToCollection} />
        );
      }

      return (
        <Header text="Waiting for public photos from Twitter..." />
      );
    }
  });

  module.exports = Stream;
```

First, we will import the following modules that our `Stream` component depends on:

- `React`: This is a React library
- `StreamTweet` and `Header`: These are React components
- `snapkite-stream-client`: This is a utility library

Then, we will define our React component. Let's take a look at the methods that our `Stream` component implements:

- `getInitialState()`
- `componentDidMount()`
- `componentWillUnmount()`
- `handleNewTweet()`
- `render()`

We're already familiar with the `getInitialState()` and `render()` methods; they are part of React's API. You already know that any React component must implement at least the `render()` method. Let's take a look at the `render()` method of our `Stream` component:

```
render: function () {
  var tweet = this.state.tweet;

  if (tweet) {
    return (
```

```
        <StreamTweet
        tweet={tweet}
        onAddTweetToCollection={this.props.onAddTweetToCollection} />
      );
    }

    return (
      <Header text="Waiting for public photos from Twitter..." />
    );
  }
```

As you can see, we created a new `tweet` variable that references the `tweet` property, which is part of a component's state object. We then check whether that variable has a reference to an actual `tweet` object, and if it does, our `render()` method returns the `StreamTweet` component, or else, it returns the `Header` component.

The `StreamTweet` component renders a header and the latest tweet from a stream, whereas the `Header` component renders only a header.

Have you noticed that our `Stream` component doesn't render anything itself, but rather returns one of the two other components that do the actual rendering? The purpose of a `Stream` component is to encapsulate our application's logic and delegate rendering to the other React components. In React, you should have at least one component that encapsulates your application's logic, stores, and manages your application's state. This is usually a root component or one of the high-level components in your component hierarchy. All the other child React components should have no state if possible. If you think of all the React components as `Views`, then our `Stream` component is a `ControllerView`.

Now that we know what a `Stream` component renders, let's discuss it in the other methods:

```
getInitialState: function () {
  return {
    tweet: null
  }
},
```

The `getInitialState()` method returns the initial state object with a `tweet` property, which is set to `null`. Our `Stream` component will receive an endless stream of new tweets, and it needs to re-render its child components every time a new tweet is received. In order to achieve this, we need to store the current tweet in the component's state. Once we update its state, React will call its `render()` method and re-render all of its child components. For this purpose, we will implement the `handleNewTweet()` method:

```
handleNewTweet: function (tweet) {
  this.setState({
    tweet: tweet
  });
},
```

The `handleNewTweet()` method takes a `tweet` object, and sets it as a new value for the component state's `tweet` property.

Where does that new tweet come from and when does it come? Let's take a look at our `componentDidMount()` method:

```
componentDidMount: function () {
  SnapkiteStreamClient.initializeStream(this.handleNewTweet);
},
```

This function calls the `initializeStream()` method of the `SnapkiteStreamClient` object, and passes a `this.handleNewTweet` callback function as its argument. `SnapkiteStreamClient` is an external library with an API that we're using to initialize a stream of tweets. The `this.handleNewTweet` function will be called for every tweet that `SnapkiteStreamClient` receives.

Why did we name this method `componentDidMount()`? We didn't. React did. In fact, the `componentDidMount()` method is part of React's API. It's one of the React component's lifecycle methods. It's called only once, immediately after React has finished the initial rendering of our component. At this point, React has created a DOM tree, which is represented by our component, and now we can access that DOM with another JavaScript library.

`componentDidMount()` is a perfect place for integrating React with another JavaScript library. This is where we connect to a stream of tweets using the external `SnapkiteStreamClient` library.

Now we know when to initialize the external JavaScript libraries in our React components, but what about the reverse process—when should we uninitialize and clean up everything that we've done in the `componentDidMount()` method? It's a good idea to clean up everything before we unmount our components. For this purpose, React API offers us another component lifecycle method— `componentWillUnmount()`:

```
componentWillUnmount: function () {
  SnapkiteStreamClient.destroyStream();
},
```

The `componentWillUnmount()` method is called by React just before React unmounts the component. As you can see in the `componentWillUnmount()` method, you're calling the `destroyStream()` method of the `SnapkiteStreamClient` object. `destroyStream()` cleans up our connection to `SnapkiteStreamClient`, and we can safely unmount our `Stream` component.

You might be wondering what are the component lifecycle methods and why do we need them?

Understanding React component's lifecycle methods

Think about what a React component does. It describes what to render. We know that it uses the `render()` method for this. However, sometimes, having only the `render()` method is not enough because what if we want to do something before or after the component has rendered? What if we want to be able to decide whether a component's `render()` method should be called at all?

Looks like what we're describing is a process during which the React component is rendered. This process has various stages, for example, before render, render, after render, and so on. In React, this process is called the **component's lifecycle**. Each React component goes through this process. What we want is a way to hook into that process, and call our own functions at different stages of that process in order to have a greater control over it. For this purpose, React provides a number of methods that we can use to get notified when a certain stage in a component's lifecycle process occurs. These methods are called the **component's lifecycle methods**. They are called in a predictable order.

All the React component's lifecycle methods can be grouped into three phases:

- **Mounting**: This phase occurs when a component is being inserted into the DOM
- **Updating**: This phase occurs when a component is being re-rendered into a virtual DOM to figure out if the actual DOM needs to be updated
- **Unmounting**: This phase occurs when a component is being removed from the DOM

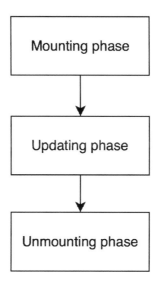

In React's terminology, inserting a component into the DOM is called "mounting", whereas removing a component from the DOM is called "unmounting".

The best way to learn about the React component's lifecycle methods is to see them in action. Let's create our `StreamTweet` component that we discussed earlier in this chapter. This component will implement most of React's lifecycle methods.

Navigate to `~/snapterest/source/components/` and create the `StreamTweet.react.js` file:

```
var React = require('react');
var ReactDOM = require('react-dom');
var Header = require('./Header.react');
var Tweet = require('./Tweet.react');

var StreamTweet = React.createClass({
```

```
    // define other component lifecycle methods here

  render: function () {
    console.log('[Snapterest] StreamTweet: Running render()');

    return (
      <section>
        <Header text={this.state.headerText} />
        <Tweet
          tweet={this.props.tweet}
          onImageClick={this.props.onAddTweetToCollection} />
      </section>
    );
  }
});

module.exports = StreamTweet;
```

As you can see, the `StreamTweet` component has no lifecycle methods yet, other than `render()`. We'll create and discuss them one by one as we move ahead.

The four methods are called during a component's *mounting* phase, as shown in the following phase:

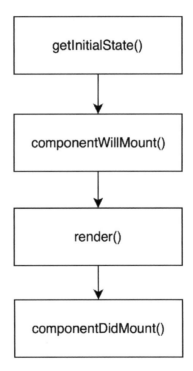

As you can see from the preceding figure, the methods called are as follows:

- `getInitialState()`
- `componentWillMount()`
- `render()`
- `componentDidMount()`

In this chapter, we'll discuss three of these four methods (except `render()`). They are called only once when the component is inserted into the DOM. Let's take a closer look at each of them.

Mounting methods

Now let's check out some of the useful mounting methods.

The getInitialState method

The `getInitialState()` method is invoked first. It is invoked *before* React inserts a component into the DOM. If you want your component to have a state, then use this method to return the initial component's state. In your `StreamTweet` component, replace this line:

```
// define other component lifecycle methods here
```

Replace the preceding line with the following code:

```
getInitialState: function () {
   console.log('[Snapterest] StreamTweet: 1. Running
getInitialState()');

   return {
     numberOfCharactersIsIncreasing: null,
     headerText: null
   };
},
```

In our `StreamTweet` component's `getInitialState()` method, we will perform the following steps:

1. Log the following message in a web browser's console:

   `[Snapterest] StreamTweet: 1. Running getInitialState().`

2. Return an object with the `numberOfCharactersIsIncreasing` and `headerText` properties set to `null`.

numberOfCharactersIsIncreasing will keep track of whether a tweet that will be displayed next has more characters in its text than a currently displayed tweet. We'll set it to a Boolean value in our next component lifecycle method.

The headerText will store the text for the Header component that StreamTweet renders.

As with all the mounting methods, getInitialState() will be called only once.

The componentWillMount method

The componentWillMount() method is invoked second. It is invoked *immediately before* React inserts a component into the DOM. Add this code right after the getInitialState() method in your StreamTweet component:

```
componentWillMount: function () {
  console.log('[Snapterest] StreamTweet: 2. Running
componentWillMount()');

  this.setState({
    numberOfCharactersIsIncreasing: true,
    headerText: 'Latest public photo from Twitter'
  });

  window.snapterest = {
    numberOfReceivedTweets: 1,
    numberOfDisplayedTweets: 1
  };
},
```

We do a number of things in this method. First, we log the fact that this method is being invoked. In fact, for the purpose of demonstration, we'll log every component lifecycle method of this component. When you run this code in a web browser, you should be able to open the JavaScript console, and see these log messages printed in the expected ascending order.

Next, we update the component's state using the this.setState() method:

- Set the numberOfCharactersIsIncreasing property to true
- Set the headerText property to 'Latest public photo from Twitter'

Because this is the very first tweet that this component will render, we know that the number of characters is definitely increasing from nothing to the number of characters in that first tweet. Hence, we set it to true. We also assign the default text to our header, 'Latest public photo from Twitter'.

As you know, calling the `this.setState()` method should trigger the component's `render()` method, so it seems like `render()` will be called twice during the component's mounting phase. However, in this case, React knows that nothing has been rendered yet, so it will call the `render()` method only once.

Finally, in this method, we define a `snapterest` global object with the following two properties:

- `numberOfReceivedTweets`: This property counts the number of all the received tweets

- `numberOfDisplayedTweets` This property counts the number of only the displayed tweets

We set `numberOfReceivedTweets` to 1 because we know that the `componentWillMount()` method is called only once when the very first tweet is received. We also know that our `render()` method will be called for this very first tweet, so we set `numberOfDisplayedTweets` to 1 as well:

```
window.snapterest = {
  numberOfReceivedTweets: 1,
  numberOfDisplayedTweets: 1
};
```

This global object is not part of React or our web application's logic; we can remove it and everything will still work as expected. `window.snapterest` is a convenience tool used to keep track of how many tweets we've processed at any point of time. We use the global `window.snapterest` object for demonstration purposes only. I would strongly advise you against adding your own properties to a global object in real life projects because you might overwrite the existing properties and/or your properties might be overwritten later by some other JavaScript code that you don't own. Later on, if you decide to deploy Snapterest in production, then make sure to remove the global `window.snapterest` object and the related code from the `StreamTweet` component.

After running Snapterest in a web browser for a few minutes, you can open the JavaScript console and type the `snapterest.numberOfReceivedTweets` and `snapterest.numberOfDisplayedTweets` commands. These commands will output the numbers that will help you get a better understanding of how fast the new tweets are coming, and how many of them are not being displayed. In our next component lifecycle method, we'll add more properties to our `window.snapterest` object.

The componentDidMount method

The `componentDidMount()` method is invoked third. It is invoked *immediately after* React inserts a component into the DOM. The updated DOM is now available for access, which means that this method is the best place for initializing other JavaScript libraries that need access to that DOM.

Earlier in this chapter, we created our `Stream` component with the `componentDidMount()` method that initializes the external `snapkite-stream-client` JavaScript library.

Let's take a look at this component's `componentDidMount()` method. Add the following code to your `StreamTweet` component after the `componentWillMount()` method:

```
componentDidMount: function () {
    console.log('[Snapterest] StreamTweet: 3. Running
componentDidMount()');

    var componentDOMRepresentation = ReactDOM.findDOMNode(this);

    window.snapterest.headerHtml = componentDOMRepresentation.
children[0].outerHTML;
    window.snapterest.tweetHtml = componentDOMRepresentation.
children[1].outerHTML;
},
```

Here, we're referencing the DOM that represents our `StreamTweet` component using the `ReactDOM.findDOMNode()` method. We pass `this` parameter that references the current component (in this case, `StreamTweet`). The `componentDOMRepresentation` variable references the DOM tree that we can traverse and access its various properties. To get a good understanding of how this DOM tree looks like, let's take a closer look at the `render()` method of our `StreamTweet` component:

```
render: function () {
    console.log('[Snapterest] StreamTweet: Running render()');

    return (
      <section>
        <Header text={this.state.headerText} />
        <Tweet
          tweet={this.props.tweet}
          onImageClick={this.props.onAddTweetToCollection} />
      </section>
    );
}
```

One of the greatest benefits of using JSX is that we can easily identify how many child elements our component will have just by looking at the component's `render()` method. Here, we can see that a parent `<section>` element has two child components: `<Header />` and `<Tweet />`.

So when we traverse the resulting DOM tree using the DOM API `children` property, we can be sure that it will have two child elements as well:

- `componentDOMRepresentation.children[0]`: This is our `<Header />` component's DOM representation
- `componentDOMRepresentation.children[1]`: This is our `<Tweet />` component's DOM representation

The `outerHTML` attribute of each element gets the HTML string that represents the DOM tree of each element. We reference this HTML string in our global `window.snapterest` object for convenience, as discussed earlier in this chapter.

If you are using another JavaScript library such as **jQuery,** along with React, then use the `componentDidMount()` method as an opportunity to integrate the two. If you want to send an AJAX request or set timers using the `setTimeout()` or `setInterval()` functions, then you can do that in this method as well. In general, `componentDidMount()` should be your preferred component lifecycle method for integrating the React library with non-React libraries and APIs.

So far, in this chapter, we've learned about the fundamental mounting methods that the React component provides us with. We used all the three of them in our `StreamTweet` component. We also discussed the `StreamTweet`'s `render()` method. This is all that we need to know to understand how React will render the `StreamTweet` component initially. On its very first render, React will execute the following sequence of methods:

1. `getInitialState()`
2. `componentWillMount()`
3. `render()`
4. `componentDidMount()`

This is called the React component's **mounting phase**. It's executed only once, unless we unmount a component and mount it again.

Next, let's discuss the React component's **unmounting phase**.

Unmounting methods

Let's now take a look at one of the popular unmounting methods.

The componentWillUnmount method

React offers only one method for this phase, that is, `componentWillUnmount()`. It is invoked *immediately before* React removes a component from the DOM and destroys it. This method is useful for cleaning up any data that is created during the component's mounting or updating phases. That's exactly what we do in our `StreamTweet` component. Add this code to your `StreamTweet` component after the `componentDidMount()` method:

```
componentWillUnmount: function () {
   console.log('[Snapterest] StreamTweet: 8. Running
componentWillUnmount()');

   delete window.snapterest;
},
```

In the `componentWillUnmount()` method, we delete our global `window.snapterest` object using the `delete` operator:

delete window.snapterest;

Removing `window.snapterest` will keep our global object clean. If you've created any additional DOM elements in the `componentDidMount()` method, then the `componentWillUnmount()` method is a good place to remove them. You can think of the `componentDidMount()` and `componentWillUnmount()` methods as a two-step mechanism for integrating the React component with another JavaScript API:

1. Initialize it in the `componentDidMount()` method
2. Terminate it in the `componentWillUnmount()` method

This way your external JavaScript libraries that need to work with the DOM will stay in sync with the DOM rendered by React.

That's all we need to know to efficiently unmount React components.

Summary

In this chapter, we created our `Stream` component and learned how to integrate a React component with the external JavaScript library. We also learned about the React component's lifecycle methods. We also focused on and discussed the mounting and unmounting methods in detail and started implementing the `StreamTweet` component.

In our next chapter, we'll take a look at the component lifecycle's updating methods. We'll also implement our `Header` and `Tweet` components, and learn how to set the component's default properties.

6

Update Your React Components

In the previous chapter, we learned that a React component can go through three phases:

- Mounting
- Updating
- Unmounting

We've already discussed the mounting and unmounting phases. In this chapter, we're going to focus on the updating phase. During this phase, a React component is already inserted into the DOM. This DOM represents a component's current state, and when that state changes, React needs to evaluate how a new state is going to mutate the previously rendered DOM.

React provides us with methods to influence what is going to be rendered during an update as well as to make us aware of when an update happens. These methods allow us to control the transition from the current component's state to the next component's state. Let's learn more about the powerful nature of the React component's updating methods.

Understanding component lifecycle's updating methods

A React component has five lifecycle methods that belong to a component's *updating* phase:

- `componentWillReceiveProps()`
- `shouldComponentUpdate()`
- `componentWillUpdate()`
- `render()`
- `componentDidUpdate()`

See the following figure for a better view:

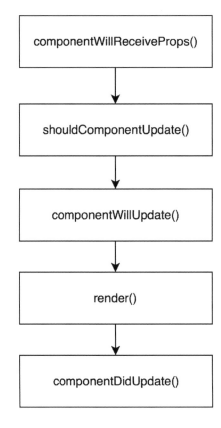

We're already familiar with the `render()` method. Now let's discuss the other four methods.

The componentWillReceiveProps method

We'll start with the componentWillReceiveProps() method in the StreamTweet component. Add the following code after the componentDidMount() method in the StreamTweet.react.js file:

```
componentWillReceiveProps: function (nextProps) {
  console.log('[Snapterest] StreamTweet: 4. Running
componentWillReceiveProps()');

  var currentTweetLength = this.props.tweet.text.length;
  var nextTweetLength = nextProps.tweet.text.length;
  var isNumberOfCharactersIncreasing = (nextTweetLength >
currentTweetLength);
  var headerText;

  this.setState({
    numberOfCharactersIsIncreasing: isNumberOfCharactersIncreasing
  });

  if (isNumberOfCharactersIncreasing) {
    headerText = 'Number of characters is increasing';
  } else {
    headerText = 'Latest public photo from Twitter';
  }

  this.setState({
    headerText: headerText
  });

  window.snapterest.numberOfReceivedTweets++;
},
```

This method is invoked first in the component lifecycle's updating phase. It is called when a component receives new properties from its parent component.

This method is an opportunity for us to compare the current component's properties using the this.props object with the next component's properties using the nextProps object. Based on this comparison, we can choose to update the component's state using the this.setState() function, which will not trigger an additional render in this scenario.

Let's see that in action:

```
var currentTweetLength = this.props.tweet.text.length;
var nextTweetLength = nextProps.tweet.text.length;
var isNumberOfCharactersIncreasing = (nextTweetLength >
currentTweetLength);
var headerText;

this.setState({
  numberOfCharactersIsIncreasing: isNumberOfCharactersIncreasing
});
```

We first get the lengths of the current tweet and the next tweet. The current one is available via `this.props.tweet` and the next one via `nextProps.tweet`. We then compare their lengths by checking whether the next tweet is longer than the current one. The result of the comparison is stored in the `isNumberOfCharactersIncreasing` variable. Finally, we update the component's state by setting the `numberOfCharactersIsIncreasing` property to the value of our `isNumberOfCharactersIncreasing` variable.

We then set our header text as follows:

```
if (isNumberOfCharactersIncreasing) {
  headerText = 'Number of characters is increasing';
} else {
  headerText = 'Latest public photo from Twitter';
}

this.setState({
  headerText: headerText
});
```

If the next tweet is longer, we set the header text to `'Number of characters is increasing'`, or else, we set it to `'Latest public photo from Twitter'`. We then update our component's state once more by setting the `headerText` property to the value of our `headerText` variable.

Notice that we call the `this.setState()` function twice in our `componentWillReceiveProps()` method. This is to illustrate the point that no matter how many times you call `this.setState()` in the `componentWillReceiveProps()` method, it won't trigger any additional renders of that component. React does an internal optimization where it batches the state updates together.

Since the `componentWillReceiveProps()` method will be called once for each new tweet that our `StreamTweet` component will receive, it makes it a good place to count the total number of the received tweets:

```
window.snapterest.numberOfReceivedTweets++;
```

Now we know how to check whether the next tweet is longer than the tweet we're currently displaying, but how can we choose not to render the next tweet at all?

The shouldComponentUpdate method

The `shouldComponentUpdate()` method allows us to decide whether the next component's state should trigger the component's re-rendering or not. This method returns a Boolean value, which by default is `true`, but you can return `false`, and the following component methods won't be called:

- `componentWillUpdate()`
- `render()`
- `componentDidUpdate()`

Skipping a call to the component's `render()` method will prevent that component from re-rendering which in turn will improve your application's performance, since no additional DOM mutations will be made.

This method is invoked second in the component lifecycle's updating phase.

This method is a great place for us to prevent the next tweet with one or less characters from being displayed. Add this code to the `StreamTweet` component after the `componentWillReceiveProps()` method:

```
shouldComponentUpdate: function (nextProps, nextState) {
  console.log('[Snapterest] StreamTweet: 5. Running
shouldComponentUpdate()');

  return (nextProps.tweet.text.length > 1);
},
```

If the next tweet's length is greater than 1, then `shouldComponentUpdate()` returns `true`, and the `StreamTweet` component renders the next tweet. Or else, it returns `false`, and the `StreamTweet` component doesn't render the next state.

The componentWillUpdate method

The componentWillUpdate() method is called *immediately before* React updates the DOM. It gets the following two arguments:

- nextProps: The next properties object
- nextState: The next state object

You can use these arguments to prepare for the DOM update. However, you cannot use this.setState() in the componentWillUpdate() method. If you want to update the component's state in response to its properties change, then do that in the componentWillReceiveProps() method, which will be called by React when the properties change.

To demonstrate when the componentWillUpdate() method is called, we need to log it in the StreamTweet component. Add this code after the shouldComponentUpdate() method:

```
componentWillUpdate: function (nextProps, nextState) {
  console.log('[Snapterest] StreamTweet: 6. Running
componentWillUpdate()');
},
```

After calling the componentWillUpdate() method, React invokes the render() method that performs the DOM update. Then, the componentDidUpdate() method is called.

The componentDidUpdate method

The componentDidUpdate() method is called *immediately after* React updates the DOM. It gets these two arguments:

- prevProps: The previous properties object
- prevState: The previous state object

We will use this method to interact with the updated DOM or perform any post-render operations. In our StreamTweet component, we'll use componentDidUpdate() to increment the number of displayed tweets in our global object. Add this code after the componentWillUpdate() method:

```
componentDidUpdate: function (prevProps, prevState) {
  console.log('[Snapterest] StreamTweet: 7. Running
componentDidUpdate()');

  window.snapterest.numberOfDisplayedTweets++;
},
```

After `componentDidUpdate()` is called, the updating cycle ends. A new cycle is started when a component's state is updated or a parent component passes new properties. Or when you call the `forceUpdate()` method, it triggers a new updating cycle, but skips the `shouldComponentUpdate()` method on a component that triggered the update. However, `shouldComponentUpdate()` is called on all the child components as per the usual updating phase. Try to avoid using the `forceUpdate()` method as much as possible; this will promote your application's maintainability.

That concludes our discussion of React component lifecycle methods.

Setting default React component properties

As you know from the previous chapter, our `StreamTweet` component renders two child components: `Header` and `Tweet`.

Let's create these components. Navigate to `~/snapterest/source/components/` and create the `Header.react.js` file:

```
var React = require('react');

var headerStyle = {
  fontSize: '16px',
  fontWeight: '300',
  display: 'inline-block',
  margin: '20px 10px'
};

var Header = React.createClass({

  getDefaultProps: function () {
    return {
      text: 'Default header'
    };
  },

  render: function () {
    return (
      <h2 style={headerStyle}>{this.props.text}</h2>
    );
  }
});

module.exports = Header;
```

As you can see, our `Header` component is a stateless component that renders the `h2` element. The header text is passed from a parent component as a `this.props.text` property, which makes this component flexible, that allows us to reuse it anywhere where we need a header. We'll reuse this component again later in this book.

Notice that the `h2` element has a `style` property.

In React, we can define the CSS rules in a JavaScript object, and then pass that object as a value to the React element's `style` property. For example, in this component, we define the `headerStyle` variable that references an object where:

- Each object key is a CSS property
- Each object value is a CSS value

The CSS properties that contain a hyphen in their names should be converted to the **CamelCase** style; for example, `font-size` becomes `fontSize`, `font-weight` becomes `fontWeight`, and so on.

The advantages of defining your CSS rules inside a React component are as follows:

- **Portability**: You can easily share a component together with its styling, all in one JavaScript file
- **Encapsulation**: Making styles inline allows you to limit the scope they affect
- **Flexibility**: The CSS rules can be calculated using the power of JavaScript

The significant disadvantage of using this technique is the fact that **Content Security Policies (CSP)** can block inline styling from having any effect. You can learn more about CSP at `https://developer.mozilla.org/en-US/docs/Web/Security/CSP/Introducing_Content_Security_Policy`.

Our `Header` component has one method that we haven't discussed yet, that is, `getDefaultProps()`. What if you forget to pass a property that a React component depends on? In that case, a component can set the default properties using the `getDefaultProps()` method, for example:

```
getDefaultProps: function () {
  return {
    text: 'Default header'
  };
},
```

In this example, we're setting a default value of `'Default header'` to our `text` property. If a parent component passes the `this.props.text` property, then it will overwrite the default one.

Next, let's create our `Tweet` component. Navigate to `~/snapterest/source/components/` and create the `Tweet.react.js` file:

```javascript
var React = require('react');

var tweetStyle = {
  position: 'relative',
  display: 'inline-block',
  width: '300px',
  height: '400px',
  margin: '10px'
};

var imageStyle = {
  maxHeight: '400px',
  boxShadow: '0px 1px 1px 0px #aaa',
  border: '1px solid #fff'
};

var Tweet = React.createClass({

  propTypes: {

    tweet: function(properties, propertyName, componentName) {

      var tweet = properties[propertyName];

      if (! tweet) {
        return new Error('Tweet must be set.');
      }

      if (! tweet.media) {
        return new Error('Tweet must have an image.');
      }
    },

    onImageClick: React.PropTypes.func
  },

  handleImageClick: function () {
    var tweet = this.props.tweet;
    var onImageClick = this.props.onImageClick;
```

```
      if (onImageClick) {
        onImageClick(tweet);
      }
    },

  render: function () {
    var tweet = this.props.tweet;
    var tweetMediaUrl = tweet.media[0].url;

    return (
      <div style={tweetStyle}>
        <img src={tweetMediaUrl} onClick={this.handleImageClick}
style={imageStyle} />
      </div>
    );
  }
});

module.exports = Tweet;
```

This component renders a `<div>` element with a child `<img>` element. Both the elements have inline styles, and the `<img>` element has a click event handler, that is, `this.handleImageClick`:

```
handleImageClick: function () {
  var tweet = this.props.tweet;
  var onImageClick = this.props.onImageClick;

  if (onImageClick) {
    onImageClick(tweet);
  }
},
```

When a user clicks on a tweet's image, the `Tweet` component checks whether a parent component has passed a `this.props.onImageClick` callback function as a property and calls that function. `this.props.onImageClick` is an optional `Tweet` component's property, so we need to check whether it was passed before we can use it. On the other hand, `tweet` is a required property.

How can we ensure that a component receives all the required properties?

Validating React component properties

In React, there is a way to validate the component properties using the component's `propTypes` object:

```
propTypes: {
  propertyName: validator
}
```

In this object, you need to specify a property name and a validator function that will determine whether a property is valid or not. React provides some predefined validators for you to reuse. They are all available in the `React.PropTypes` object:

- `React.PropTypes.number`: This will validate whether a property is a number or not

- `React.PropTypes.string`: This will validate whether a property is a string or not

- `React.PropTypes.bool`: This will validate whether a property is a Boolean or not

- `React.PropTypes.object`: This will validate whether a property is an object or not

- `React.PropTypes.element`: This will validate whether a property is a React element or not

For a complete list of the `React.PropTypes` validators, you can check the docs at `https://facebook.github.io/react/docs/reusable-components.html#prop-validation`.

By default, all the properties that you validate with the `React.PropTypes` validators are optional. You can chain any of them with `isRequired` to make sure that a warning message is displayed on a JavaScript console when a property is missing:

```
propTypes: {
  propertyName: React.PropTypes.number.isRequired
}
```

You can also specify your own custom validator function that should return an `Error` object if the validation fails:

```
propTypes: {
  propertyName: function (properties, propertyName, componentName) {
    // ... validation failed
    return new Error('A property is not valid.');
  }
}
```

Let's take a look at the `propTypes` object in our `Tweet` component:

```
propTypes: {

  tweet: function(properties, propertyName, componentName) {

    var tweet = properties[propertyName];

    if (! tweet) {
      return new Error('Tweet must be set.');
    }

    if (! tweet.media) {
      return new Error('Tweet must have an image.');
    }
  },

  onImageClick: React.PropTypes.func
},
```

As you can see, we're validating two `Tweet` component properties: `tweet` and `onImageClick`.

We use the custom validator function to validate the `tweet` property. React passes three parameters to this function:

- `properties`: This is the component properties object
- `propertyName`: This is the name of the property that we're validating
- `componentName`: This is the name of the component

We first check whether our `Tweet` component received the `tweet` property:

```
var tweet = properties[propertyName];

if (! tweet) {
  return new Error('Tweet must be set.');
}
```

Then, we assume that the `tweet` property is an object, and check whether that object has no `media` property:

```
if (! tweet.media) {
  return new Error('Tweet must have an image.');
}
```

Both of these checks return an `Error` object that will be logged in a JavaScript console.

Another `Tweet` component's property that we will validate is `onImageClick`:

```
onImageClick: React.PropTypes.func
```

We validate that the value of the `onImageClick` property is a function. In this case, we reuse a validator function provided by the `React.PropTypes` object. As you can see, `onImageClick` is an optional property because we didn't add `isRequired`.

Finally, for performance reasons, `propTypes` is only checked in the development version of React.

Creating a Collection component

You might recall that our topmost hierarchy `Application` component has two child components: `Stream` and `Collection`.

So far, we've discussed and implemented our `Stream` component and its child components. Next, we're going to focus on our `Collection` component.

Create the `~/snapterest/source/components/Collection.react.js` file:

```
var React = require('react');
var ReactDOMServer = require('react-dom/server');
var CollectionControls = require('./CollectionControls.react');
var TweetList = require('./TweetList.react');
var Header = require('./Header.react');

var Collection = React.createClass({

  createHtmlMarkupStringOfTweetList: function () {
    var htmlString = ReactDOMServer.renderToStaticMarkup(
      <TweetList tweets={this.props.tweets} />
    );

    var htmlMarkup = {
      html: htmlString
    };

    return JSON.stringify(htmlMarkup);
  },
  getListOfTweetIds: function () {
    return Object.keys(this.props.tweets);
```

```
  },

  getNumberOfTweetsInCollection: function () {
    return this.getListOfTweetIds().length;
  },

  render: function () {
    var numberOfTweetsInCollection = this.
getNumberOfTweetsInCollection();

    if (numberOfTweetsInCollection > 0) {

      var tweets = this.props.tweets;
      var htmlMarkup = this.createHtmlMarkupStringOfTweetList();
      var removeAllTweetsFromCollection = this.props.
onRemoveAllTweetsFromCollection;
      var handleRemoveTweetFromCollection = this.props.
onRemoveTweetFromCollection;

      return (
        <div>

          <CollectionControls
            numberOfTweetsInCollection={numberOfTweetsInCollection}
            htmlMarkup={htmlMarkup}
onRemoveAllTweetsFromCollection={removeAllTweetsFromCollection} />

          <TweetList
            tweets={tweets}
            onRemoveTweetFromCollection={handleRemoveTweetFromCollect
ion} />

        </div>
      );
    }

    return <Header text="Your collection is empty" />;
  }
});

module.exports = Collection;
```

Our `Collection` component is responsible for rendering two things:

- Tweets that a user has collected
- User interface control elements for manipulating that collection

Let's take a look at the component's `render()` method:

```
render: function () {
  var numberOfTweetsInCollection = this.
getNumberOfTweetsInCollection();

  if (numberOfTweetsInCollection > 0) {

    var tweets = this.props.tweets;
    var htmlMarkup = this.createHtmlMarkupStringOfTweetList();
    var removeAllTweetsFromCollection = this.props.
onRemoveAllTweetsFromCollection;
    var handleRemoveTweetFromCollection = this.props.
onRemoveTweetFromCollection;

    return (
      <div>

        <CollectionControls
          numberOfTweetsInCollection={numberOfTweetsInCollection}
          htmlMarkup={htmlMarkup}
          onRemoveAllTweetsFromCollection={removeAllTweetsFromCollect
ion} />

        <TweetList
          tweets={tweets}
          onRemoveTweetFromCollection={handleRemoveTweetFromCollecti
on} />

      </div>
    );
  }

  return <Header text="Your collection is empty" />;
}
```

We first get a number of tweets in the collection using the `this.`
`getNumberOfTweetsInCollection()` method:

```
getNumberOfTweetsInCollection: function () {
  return this.getListOfTweetIds().length;
},
```

This method in turn uses another method to get a list of tweet IDs:

```
getListOfTweetIds: function () {
  return Object.keys(this.props.tweets);
},
```

The `this.getListOfTweetIds()` function call returns an array of tweet IDs,
and then `this.getNumberOfTweetsInCollection()` returns a length of that array.

In our `render()` method, once we know the number of tweets in our collection,
we have to make a choice:

- If the collection is *not* empty, then render the `CollectionControls` and
  `TweetList` components
- Otherwise, render the `Header` component

What do all these components render?

- The `CollectionControls` component renders a header with a collection
  name and a set of buttons that allow users to rename, empty, and export
  a collection
- The `TweetList` component renders a list of tweets
- The `Header` component simply renders a header with a message that the
  collection is empty

The idea is to only show a collection when it's not empty. In that case, we're creating
four variables:

```
var tweets = this.props.tweets;
var htmlMarkup = this.createHtmlMarkupStringOfTweetList();
var removeAllTweetsFromCollection = this.props.
onRemoveAllTweetsFromCollection;
var handleRemoveTweetFromCollection = this.props.
onRemoveTweetFromCollection;
```

- The `tweets` variable references our `tweets` property that is passed from a
  parent component

- The `htmlMarkup` variable references a string that is returned by the component's `this.createHtmlMarkupStringOfTweetList()` method

- The `removeAllTweetsFromCollection` and `handleRemoveTweetFromCollection` variables reference functions that are passed from a parent component

As the name suggests, the `this.createHtmlMarkupStringOfTweetList()` method creates a string that represents the HTML markup created by rendering the `TweetList` component:

```
createHtmlMarkupStringOfTweetList: function () {
  var htmlString = ReactDOMServer.renderToStaticMarkup(
    <TweetList tweets={this.props.tweets} />
  );

  var htmlMarkup = {
    html: htmlString
  };

  return JSON.stringify(htmlMarkup);
},
```

The `createHtmlMarkupStringOfTweetList()` function uses the `ReactDOMServer.renderToStaticMarkup()` method that we discussed in *Chapter 2, Create Your First React Element*. We pass the `TweetList` component as its argument:

```
var htmlString = ReactDOMServer.renderToStaticMarkup(
  <TweetList tweets={this.props.tweets} />
);
```

This `TweetList` component has a `tweets` property that references the `tweets` property passed by a parent component.

The resulting HTML string produced by the `ReactDOMServer.renderToStaticMarkup()` function is stored in the `htmlString` variable. Then, we create a new `htmlMarkup` object with the `html` property that references our `htmlString` variable. Finally, we use the `JSON.stringify()` function to convert our `htmlMarkup` JavaScript object to a JSON string. The result of the `JSON.stringify(htmlMarkup)` call is what our `createHtmlMarkupStringOfTweetList()` function returns.

This method demonstrates how flexible React components are; you can use the same React components to render the DOM elements as well as produce a string of HTML markup that can be passed to a third-party API.

Another interesting observation that one can make is the use of JSX syntax outside a render() method. In fact, you can use JSX anywhere in your source file, even outside the React.createClass() function.

Let's take a closer look at what the Collection component returns when our collection is *not* empty:

```
return (
  <div>

    <CollectionControls
      numberOfTweetsInCollection={numberOfTweetsInCollection}
      htmlMarkup={htmlMarkup}
onRemoveAllTweetsFromCollection={removeAllTweetsFromCollection} />

    <TweetList
      tweets={tweets}
      onRemoveTweetFromCollection={handleRemoveTweetFromCollection} />

  </div>
);
```

We wrap the CollectionControls and TweetList components in the `<div>` element because React allows only one root element. Let's take a look at each component and discuss its properties.

We pass the following three properties to the CollectionControls component:

- The numberOfTweetsInCollection property references the current number of tweets in our collection.

- The htmlMarkup property references a string of HTML markup that we produce in this component using the createHtmlMarkupStringOfTweetList() method.

- The onRemoveAllTweetsFromCollection property references a function that removes all the tweets from our collection. This function is implemented in the Application component as discussed in *Chapter 4, Make Your React Components Reactive*.

We pass these two properties to the TweetList component:

- The tweets property references tweets passed from a parent Application component.

- The onRemoveTweetFromCollection property references a function that removes a tweet from a collection of tweets that we store in the Application component's state. We've already discussed this function in *Chapter 4, Make Your React Components Reactive*.

That's our Collection component.

Summary

In this chapter, we learned about a component's lifecycle updating methods. We also discussed how to validate the component properties and set the default properties. We also made good progress with our Snapterest application; we created and discussed the Header, Tweet, and Collection components.

In the next chapter, we'll focus on building more complex React components and finish building our Snapterest application!

7
Build Complex React Components

In this chapter, we'll put everything we learned so far about React components in action by building the most complex components in our application, that is, child components of our `Collection` component. Our aim in this chapter is to gain a solid React experience and grow our React muscle. Let's get started!

Creating the TweetList component

As you know, our `Collection` component has two child components: `CollectionControls` and `TweetList`.

We'll first build the `TweetList` component. Create the following `~/snapterest/source/components/TweetList.react.js` file:

```
var React = require('react');
var Tweet = require('./Tweet.react.js');

var listStyle = {
  padding: '0'
};

var listItemStyle = {
  display: 'inline-block',
  listStyle: 'none'
};

var TweetList = React.createClass({
```

```
    getListOfTweetIds: function () {
      return Object.keys(this.props.tweets);
    },

  getTweetElement: function (tweetId) {
      var tweet = this.props.tweets[tweetId];
      var handleRemoveTweetFromCollection = this.props.
onRemoveTweetFromCollection;
      var tweetElement;

      if (handleRemoveTweetFromCollection) {
        tweetElement = (
          <Tweet
            tweet={tweet}
            onImageClick={handleRemoveTweetFromCollection} />
        );
      } else {
        tweetElement = <Tweet tweet={tweet} />;
      }

      return <li style={listItemStyle} key={tweet.id}>{tweetElement}</
li>;
    },

  render: function () {
      var tweetElements = this.getListOfTweetIds().map(this.
getTweetElement);

      return (
        <ul style={listStyle}>
          {tweetElements}
        </ul>
      );
    }
});

module.exports = TweetList;
```

The TweetList component renders a list of tweets using the render function:

```
render: function () {
  var tweetElements = this.getListOfTweetIds().map(this.
getTweetElement);

  return (
```

```
      <ul style={listStyle}>
        {tweetElements}
      </ul>
    );
  }
```

First, we create a list of `Tweet` elements:

```
var tweetElements = this.getListOfTweetIds().map(this.
getTweetElement);
```

The `this.getListOfTweetIds()` method returns an array of tweet IDs:

```
getListOfTweetIds: function () {
  return Object.keys(this.props.tweets);
},
```

Then, for each tweet ID in that array, we create a `Tweet` component. For this, we will call the `map()` method on our array of tweet IDs and pass the `this.getTweetElement` method as a callback function:

```
getTweetElement: function (tweetId) {
  var tweet = this.props.tweets[tweetId];
  var handleRemoveTweetFromCollection = this.props.
onRemoveTweetFromCollection;
  var tweetElement;

  if (handleRemoveTweetFromCollection) {
    tweetElement = (
      <Tweet
        tweet={tweet}
        onImageClick={handleRemoveTweetFromCollection} />
    );
  } else {
    tweetElement = <Tweet tweet={tweet} />;
  }

  return <li style={listItemStyle} key={tweet.id}>{tweetElement}</li>;
},
```

The `getTweetElement()` method returns a `Tweet` element wrapped in the `<li>` element. As we already know that the `Tweet` component has an optional `onImageClick` property. When do we want to provide this optional property and when don't we?

There are two scenarios. In the first scenario, the user will click on a tweet image to remove it from a collection of tweets. In this scenario, our `Tweet` component will react to a `click` event, so we need to provide the `onImageClick` property. In the second scenario, the user will export a static collection of tweets that has no user interaction. In this scenario, we don't need to provide the `onImageClick` property.

That's exactly what we do in our `getTweetElement()` method:

```
var tweet = this.props.tweets[tweetId];
var handleRemoveTweetFromCollection = this.props.
onRemoveTweetFromCollection;
var tweetElement;

if (handleRemoveTweetFromCollection) {
  tweetElement = (
    <Tweet
      tweet={tweet}
      onImageClick={handleRemoveTweetFromCollection} />
  );
} else {
  tweetElement = <Tweet tweet={tweet} />;
}
```

We create a `tweet` variable that stores a tweet with an ID that is provided by the `tweetId` argument. Then, we create a variable that stores a `this.props.onRemoveTweetFromCollection` property that is passed by a parent `Collection` component.

Next, we check whether the `this.props.onRemoveTweetFromCollection` property is provided by a `Collection` component. If it is, then we create a `Tweet` component with an `onImageClick` property:

```
tweetElement = (
  <Tweet
    tweet={tweet}
    onImageClick={handleRemoveTweetFromCollection} />
);
```

If it isn't provided, then we create a `Tweet` component without a `handleImageClick` property:

```
tweetElement = <Tweet tweet={tweet} />;
```

We use the `TweetList` component in the following two cases:

- This component is used when rendering a collection of tweets in the `Collection` component. In this case, the `onRemoveTweetFromCollection` property *is* provided.

- This component is used when rendering a string of HTML markup that represents a collection of tweets in the `Collection` component. In this case, the `onRemoveTweetFromCollection` property *is not* provided.

Once we create our `Tweet` element, and put it into the `tweetElement` variable, we return the `<li>` element with an inline style:

```
return <li style={listItemStyle} key={tweet.id}>{tweetElement}</li>;
```

Besides the `style` property, our `<li>` element has a `key` property. It is used by React to identify each child element that is created dynamically. I recommend that you read more about dynamic children at `https://facebook.github.io/react/docs/multiple-components.html#dynamic-children`.

That's how the `getTweetElement()` method works. As a result, the `TweetList` component returns an unordered list of `Tweet` elements:

```
return (
  <ul style={listStyle}>
    {tweetElements}
  </ul>
);
```

Creating the CollectionControls component

Now, when we understand what the `Collection` component renders, let's discuss its child components. We'll start with `CollectionControls`. Create the following `~/snapterest/source/components/CollectionControls.react.js` file:

```
var React = require('react');
var Header = require('./Header.react');
var Button = require('./Button.react');
var CollectionRenameForm = require('./CollectionRenameForm.react');
var CollectionExportForm = require('./CollectionExportForm.react');

var CollectionControls = React.createClass({
```

```
getInitialState: function () {
  return {
    name: 'new',
    isEditingName: false
  };
},

getHeaderText: function () {
  var numberOfTweetsInCollection = this.props.
numberOfTweetsInCollection;
  var text = numberOfTweetsInCollection;

  if (numberOfTweetsInCollection === 1) {
    text = text + ' tweet in your';
  } else {
    text = text + ' tweets in your';
  }

  return (
    <span>
      {text} <strong>{this.state.name}</strong> collection
    </span>
  );
},

toggleEditCollectionName: function () {
  this.setState({
    isEditingName: !this.state.isEditingName
  });
},

setCollectionName: function (name) {
  this.setState({
    name: name,
    isEditingName: false
  });
},

render: function () {

  if (this.state.isEditingName) {
    return (
      <CollectionRenameForm
        name={this.state.name}
```

```
                  onChangeCollectionName={this.setCollectionName}
                  onCancelCollectionNameChange={this.toggleEditCollectionName}
      />
          );
        }

        return (
          <div>
            <Header text={this.getHeaderText()} />

            <Button
              label="Rename collection"
              handleClick={this.toggleEditCollectionName} />

            <Button
              label="Empty collection"
              handleClick={this.props.onRemoveAllTweetsFromCollection} />

            <CollectionExportForm htmlMarkup={this.props.htmlMarkup} />
          </div>
        );
      }
    });

    module.exports = CollectionControls;
```

The `CollectionControls` component, as the name suggests, renders a user interface to control a collection. These controls allow the user to:

- Rename a collection
- Empty a collection
- Export a collection

A collection has a name. By default, this name is `new` and users can change it. A collection name is displayed in a header that is rendered by the `CollectionControls` component. This component is a perfect candidate for storing the collection's name, and since changing a name will require a component re-render, we'll store that name in the component's state object:

```
getInitialState: function () {
  return {
    name: 'new',
    isEditingName: false
  };
},
```

The `CollectionControls` component can render either collection control elements or a form to change the collection name. A user can switch between the two. We need a way to represent these two states—we'll use the `isEditingName` property for that purpose. By default, `isEditingName` is set to `false`; and therefore, users won't see a form to change the collection name, when the `CollectionControls` component is mounted. Let's take a look at its `render()` method:

```
render: function () {

  if (this.state.isEditingName) {
    return (
      <CollectionRenameForm
        name={this.state.name}
        onChangeCollectionName={this.setCollectionName}
        onCancelCollectionNameChange={this.toggleEditCollectionName}
 />
    );
  }

  return (
    <div>
      <Header text={this.getHeaderText()} />

      <Button
        label="Rename collection"
        handleClick={this.toggleEditCollectionName} />

      <Button
        label="Empty collection"
        handleClick={this.props.onRemoveAllTweetsFromCollection} />

      <CollectionExportForm htmlMarkup={this.props.htmlMarkup} />
    </div>
  );
}
```

First, we check whether the component state's property `this.state.isEditingName` is set to `true`. If it is, then the `CollectionControls` component returns the `CollectionRenameForm` component that renders a form to change the collection name:

```
<CollectionRenameForm
  name={this.state.name}
  onChangeCollectionName={this.setCollectionName}
  onCancelCollectionNameChange={this.toggleEditCollectionName} />
```

The `CollectionRenameForm` component renders a form to change the collection name. It receives three properties:

- The `name` property references the current collection name
- The `onChangeCollectionName` and `onCancelCollectionNameChange` properties reference the component's methods

We'll implement the `CollectionRenameForm` component later in this chapter. Now let's take a closer look at the `setCollectionName` method:

```
setCollectionName: function (name) {
  this.setState({
    name: name,
    isEditingName: false
  });
},
```

The `setCollectionName()` function updates the collection's name and hides a form to edit the collection name by updating the component's state. We'll call this method when the user submits a new collection name.

Now, let's take a look at the `toggleEditCollectionName()` method:

```
toggleEditCollectionName: function () {
  this.setState({
    isEditingName: !this.state.isEditingName
  });
},
```

It shows or hides the collection's name editing form by setting the `isEditingName` property to the opposite of its current Boolean value using the `!` operator. We'll call this method when the user clicks on the **Rename collection** or **Cancel** buttons, that is, show or hide the collection name change form.

If the `CollectionControls` component state's property `this.state.isEditingName` is set to `false`, then it returns collection controls:

```
return (
  <div>
    <Header text={this.getHeaderText()} />

    <Button
      label="Rename collection"
      handleClick={this.toggleEditCollectionName} />
```

```
  <Button
    label="Empty collection"
    handleClick={this.props.onRemoveAllTweetsFromCollection} />

  <CollectionExportForm htmlMarkup={this.props.htmlMarkup} />
</div>
);
```

We wrap the `Header` component, two `Button` components, and the
`CollectionExportForm` component in a `div` element. You're already familiar
with a `Header` component from the previous chapter. It receives a `text` property
that references a string. However, in this case, we do not directly pass a string,
but rather a call to the `this.getHeaderText()` function:

```
<Header text={this.getHeaderText()} />
```

In turn, `this.getHeaderText()` returns a string. Let's take a closer look at
`this.getHeaderText()`:

```
getHeaderText: function () {
  var numberOfTweetsInCollection = this.props.
numberOfTweetsInCollection;
  var text = numberOfTweetsInCollection;

  if (numberOfTweetsInCollection === 1) {
    text = text + ' tweet in your';
  } else {
    text = text + ' tweets in your';
  }

  return (
    <span>
      {text} <strong>{this.state.name}</strong> collection
    </span>
  );
},
```

This method generates a string for a header based on the number of tweets in our
collection. The important feature of this method is that it returns not only a string,
but rather a tree of React elements that encapsulate that string. First, we create the
`numberOfTweetsInCollection` variable. It stores a number of tweets in a collection.
We then create a `text` variable and assign it a number of tweets in a collection. At
this point, the `text` variable stores an integer value. Our next task is to concatenate
the right string to it based on what that integer value is:

- If `numberOfTweetsInCollection` is 1, then we need to concatenate `' tweet
  in your'`

- Otherwise, we need to concatenate `' tweets in your'`

Once the header string is created, then we return the following elements:

```
return (
  <span>
    {text} <strong>{this.state.name}</strong> collection
  </span>
);
```

The final string encapsulated inside a `<span>` element consists of a value of a `text` variable, a collection name, and the `collection` keyword. For example, run the following command:

```
1 tweet in your new collection.
```

Once this string is returned by the `getHeaderText()` method, it is then passed as a property to a `Header` component. Our next collection control element in the `CollectionControls`'s `render()` method is `Button`:

```
<Button
  label="Rename collection"
  handleClick={this.toggleEditCollectionName} />
```

We pass the `Rename collection` string to its `label` property and the `this.toggleEditCollectionName` method to its `handleClick` property. As a result, this button will have the `Rename collection` label, and it will toggle a form to change the collection name.

The next collection control element is our second `Button`:

```
<Button
  label="Empty collection"
  handleClick={this.props.onRemoveAllTweetsFromCollection} />
```

As you can guess, it will have an `Empty collection` label, and it will remove all the tweets from a collection.

Our final collection control element is `CollectionExportForm`:

```
<CollectionExportForm htmlMarkup={this.props.htmlMarkup} />
```

It receives an HTML markup string that represents our collection, and it will render a button. We'll create this component later in this chapter.

Now, when we understand what the `CollectionControls` component will render, let's take a closer look at its child components. We'll start with the `CollectionRenameForm` component.

Creating the CollectionRenameForm component

First, let's create the ~/snapterest/source/components/CollectionRenameForm. react.js file:

```
var React = require('react');
var ReactDOM = require('react-dom');
var Header = require('./Header.react');
var Button = require('./Button.react');

var inputStyle = {
  marginRight: '5px'
};

var CollectionRenameForm = React.createClass({

  getInitialState: function() {
    return {
      inputValue: this.props.name
    };
  },

  setInputValue: function (inputValue) {
    this.setState({
      inputValue: inputValue
    });
  },

  handleInputValueChange: function (event) {
    var inputValue = event.target.value;
    this.setInputValue(inputValue);
  },

  handleFormSubmit: function (event) {
    event.preventDefault();

    var collectionName = this.state.inputValue;
    this.props.onChangeCollectionName(collectionName);
  },

  handleFormCancel: function (event) {
    event.preventDefault();
```

```
      var collectionName = this.props.name;
      this.setInputValue(collectionName);
      this.props.onCancelCollectionNameChange();
    },

    componentDidMount: function () {
      this.refs.collectionName.focus();
    },

    render: function () {
      return (
        <form className="form-inline" onSubmit={this.handleSubmit}>

          <Header text="Collection name:" />

          <div className="form-group">
            <input
              className="form-control"
              style={inputStyle}
              onChange={this.handleInputValueChange}
              value={this.state.inputValue}
              ref="collectionName" />
          </div>

          <Button label="Change" handleClick={this.handleFormSubmit} />
          <Button label="Cancel" handleClick={this.handleFormCancel} />
        </form>
      );
    }
});

module.exports = CollectionRenameForm;
```

This component renders a form to change the collection name:

```
render: function () {
  return (
    <form className="form-inline" onSubmit={this.handleSubmit}>

      <Header text="Collection name:" />

      <div className="form-group">
        <input
          className="form-control"
          style={inputStyle}
```

```
            onChange={this.handleInputValueChange}
            value={this.state.inputValue}
            ref="collectionName" />
        </div>

        <Button label="Change" handleClick={this.handleFormSubmit} />
        <Button label="Cancel" handleClick={this.handleFormCancel} />
      </form>
    );
}
```

Our `<form>` element wraps four elements, which are as follows:

- One `Header` component
- One `<input>` element
- Two `Button` components

The `Header` component renders the `'Collection name:'` string. The `<input>` element is wrapped inside a `<div>` element with a `className` property set to `form-group`. This name is part of the Bootstrap framework that we discussed in *Chapter 4, Make Your React Components Reactive*. It's used for layout and styling and it's not part of our React application's logic.

The `<input>` element has quite a few properties. Let's take a closer look at it:

```
<input
  className="form-control"
  style={inputStyle}
  onChange={this.handleInputValueChange}
  value={this.state.inputValue}
  ref="collectionName" />
```

- The `className` property is set to `form-control`. It is another class name, which is part of the Bootstrap framework. We will use this for styling purposes.

- In addition, we apply our own style to this `input` element using the `style` property that references the `inputStyle` object with a single style rule, that is, `marginRight`.

- The `value` property is set to a current value stored in the component's state, `this.state.inputValue`.

- The `onChange` property references a `this.handleInputValueChange` method that is an `onchange` event handler.

- `ref` is a special React property that you can attach to any component that is returned by a `render()` method. It allows you to refer to that component outside a `render()` method. Shortly, we'll see an example of this.

I would like you to focus on the last three properties: `value`, `onChange`, and `ref`. The `value` property is set to the component state's property, and the only way to change that value is to update its state. On the other hand, we know that a user can interact with an input field and change its value. Will this behavior apply to our component? No. Whenever a user types, our input field's value won't change. This is because a component is in control of `<input>`, not a user. In our `CollectionRenameForm` component, the value of the `<input>` always reflects the value of the `this.state.inputValue` property, regardless of what the user types. The user is not in control, but the `CollectionRenameForm` component is.

Then, how can we make sure that our input field reacts to a user input? We need to listen to a user input, and update the state of the `CollectionRenameForm` component, which in turn will re-render the input field with an updated value. Doing so on every input's `change` event will make our input look like it works as usual, and the user can freely change its value.

For this, we provide our `<input>` element with the `onChange` property that references the component's `this.handleInputValueChange` method:

```
handleInputValueChange: function (event) {
  var inputValue = event.target.value;
  this.setInputValue(inputValue);
},
```

As we discussed in *Chapter 3, Create Your First React Component*, React passes instances of `SyntheticEvent` to event handlers. The `handleInputValueChange()` method receives an `event` object with a `target` property that has a `value` property. This `value` property stores a string that a user has typed in our input field. We pass that string into our `this.setInputValue()` method:

```
setInputValue: function (inputValue) {
  this.setState({
    inputValue: inputValue
  });
},
```

`setInputValue()` is a convenient method that updates the component's state with a new input value. In turn, this update will re-render the `<input>` element with an updated value.

What's the initial input's value when the `CollectionRenameForm` component is mounted? Let's take a look at this:

```
getInitialState: function() {
  return {
    inputValue: this.props.name
  };
},
```

As you can see, we pass the collection's name from a parent component, and we use it to set our initial input value.

After we mount this component, we want to set focus on the input field so that the user can start editing the collection's name straightaway. We know that once a component is inserted into the DOM, React calls its `componentDidMount()` method. This method is our best opportunity to set focus:

```
componentDidMount: function () {
  this.refs.collectionName.focus();
},
```

To do this, we get our input element and call the `focus()` function on it.

How can we reference an element inside the `componentDidMount()` method? We can use the `this.refs` object to refer to our `input` element. Because we provided our `input` element with a `ref` property, which is set to `collectionName`, we can refer to it via `this.refs.collectionName`.

Finally, let's discuss our two form buttons:

- The `Change` button submits the form and changes the collection name
- The `Cancel` button submits the form but doesn't change the collection name

We'll start with a `Change` button:

```
<Button label="Change" handleClick={this.handleFormSubmit} />
```

When a user clicks on it, the `this.handleFormSubmit` method is called:

```
handleFormSubmit: function (event) {
  event.preventDefault();

  var collectionName = this.state.inputValue;
  this.props.onChangeCollectionName(collectionName);
},
```

We cancel the `submit` event, then get the collection name from the component's state, and pass it to the `this.props.onChangeCollectionName()` function call. The `onChangeCollectionName` function is passed by a parent `CollectionControls` component. Calling this function will change our collection's name.

Now let's discuss our second form button:

```
<Button label="Cancel" handleClick={this.handleFormCancel} />
```

When a user clicks on it, the `this.handleFormCancel` method is called:

```
handleFormCancel: function (event) {
  event.preventDefault();

  var collectionName = this.props.name;
  this.setInputValue(collectionName);
  this.props.onCancelCollectionNameChange();
},
```

Once again, we cancel a `submit` event, then get the original collection name that is passed as a property by a parent `CollectionControls` component, and pass it to our `this.setInputValue()` function. Then, we call the `this.props.onCancelCollectionNameChange()` function that hides the collection controls.

That's our `CollectionRenameForm` component. Next, let's create our `Button` component that we reused twice in our `CollectionRenameForm` component.

Creating the Button component

Create the following `~/snapterest/source/components/Button.react.js` file:

```
var React = require('react');

var buttonStyle = {
  margin: '10px 10px 10px 0'
};

var Button = React.createClass({
  render: function () {
    return (
      <button
        className="btn btn-default"
        style={buttonStyle}
        onClick={this.props.handleClick}>{this.props.label}</button>
    );
```

```
  }
});
```

```
module.exports = Button;
```

The `Button` component renders a button. You might be wondering what's the benefit of creating a dedicated component for a button if you could just use the `<button>` element? Think of a component as a wrapper for a `<button>` element and something else that comes with it. In our case, most `<button>` elements come with the same style, so it makes sense to encapsulate both the `<button>` and style objects inside a component, and reuse that component. Hence, the `Button` component. It expects to receive two properties from a parent component:

- The `label` property is a label for a button
- The `handleClick` property is a callback function that is called when a user clicks on this button

Now, it's time to create our `CollectionExportForm` component.

Creating the CollectionExportForm component

The `CollectionExportForm` component is responsible for exporting a collection to a third-party website (`http://CodePen.io`). Once your collection is on CodePen, you can save it and share it with your friends. Let's take a look at how this can be done.

Create the `~/snapterest/source/components/CollectionExportForm.react.js` file:

```
var React = require('react');

var formStyle = {
  display: 'inline-block'
};

var CollectionExportForm = React.createClass({
  render: function () {
    return (
      <form action="http://codepen.io/pen/define" method="POST"
target="_blank" style={formStyle}>
        <input type="hidden" name="data" value={this.props.htmlMarkup}
/>
```

```
        <button type="submit" className="btn btn-default">Export as
HTML</button>
      </form>
    );
  }
});

module.exports = CollectionExportForm;
```

The `CollectionExportForm` component renders a form with the `<input>` and `<button>` elements. The `<input>` element is hidden, and its value is set to an HTML markup string that is passed by a parent component. The `<button>` element is the only element in this form that is visible to a user. When a user clicks on the **Export as HTML** button, a collection is submitted to CodePen.io that is opened in a new window. A user can then modify and share that collection.

Congratulations! At this point, we've built a fully functional web application with React. Let's see how it works.

First, make sure that the Snapkite Engine that we installed and configured in *Chapter 1*, *Installing Powerful Tools for Your Project*, is running. Navigate to `~/snapkite-engine/` and run the following command:

npm start

Then, open a new Terminal window, navigate to `~/snapterest/`, and run this command:

gulp

Now open `~/snapterest/build/index.html` in your web browser. You will see new tweets appear. Click on them to add them to your collection. Click on them again to remove individual tweets from the collection. Click on the **Empty collection** button to remove all the tweets from your collection. Click on the **Rename collection** button, type a new collection name, and click on the **Change** button. Finally, click on the **Export as HTML** button to export your collection to CodePen.io. If you have any trouble with this chapter or previous chapters, then go to `https://github.com/fedosejev/react-essentials` and create a new issue.

Summary

In this chapter, you created the `TweetList`, `CollectionControls`, `CollectionRenameForm`, `CollectionExportForm`, and `Button` components. You completed building a fully functional React application. In our next chapters, we'll test it with Jest and enhance it with Flux.

8
Test Your React Application with Jest

By now, you must have created a number of React components. Some of them are quite straightforward, but some are sophisticated enough. Having built both, you might have gained a certain confidence, which makes you believe that no matter how complex the user interface is you can build it with React, without any major pitfalls. This is a good confidence to have. After all that's why we're investing time in learning React. However, there is a trap that many confident React developers fall into; the act of not writing unit tests.

What is a unit test? As the name suggests, it's a test for a single unit of your application. A single unit in your application is often a function, which suggests that writing unit tests means writing tests for your functions.

Why write unit tests?

You might be wondering why you should write unit tests? Let me tell you a story from my personal experience. I had a release of a new website that I built recently. A few days later, my colleague who was using the website sent me an e-mail with a few files that the website would reject. I closely examined the files, and the requirement of having the IDs matched in both of them was met. However, the files were still rejected, and the error message said that the IDs didn't match. Can you guess what the problem was?

I wrote a function that will check whether the IDs from the two files match. The function checked both the value and the type of an ID, so even if the values were the same and the types were different, it would return no match. Turns out, that was exactly the case with the files from my colleague. The important question is how could I prevent this from happening? The answer is a number of unit tests for my function.

Creating test suits, specs, and expectations

How does one write a test for JavaScript functions? You need a testing framework, and luckily, Facebook has built its own unit test framework for JavaScript called **Jest**. It is built on top of **Jasmine**; another well-known JavaScript test framework. Those of you who are familiar with Jasmine will find Jest's approach to testing very similar. However, I'll make no assumptions about your prior experience with testing frameworks and discuss the basics first.

The fundamental idea of unit testing is that you test only one piece of functionality in your application that usually is implemented by one function. You test it in isolation, which means that all the other parts of your application that the function depends on are not used by your tests. Instead, they are imitated by your tests. To imitate a JavaScript object is to create a fake one that simulates the behavior of the real object. In unit testing, the fake object is called **mock** and the process of creating it is called **mocking**.

Jest automatically mocks the dependencies when you're running your tests. It automatically finds tests to be executed in your repository. Let's take a look at the following example.

First, create the `~/snapterest/source/utils/` directory. Then, create a new `TweetUtils.js` file in it:

```
function getListOfTweetIds(tweets) {
  return Object.keys(tweets);
}

module.exports.getListOfTweetIds = getListOfTweetIds;
```

The `TweetUtils.js` file is a module with the `getListOfTweetIds()` utility function for our application to use. Given an object with tweets, `getListOfTweetIds()` returns an array of tweet IDs. Using the CommonJS module pattern, we will export this function:

```
module.exports.getListOfTweetIds = getListOfTweetIds;
```

Now let's write our first unit test with Jest. We'll test our `getListOfTweetIds()` function.

Create a new directory: `~/snapterest/source/utils/__tests__/`. Jest will run any tests in any `__tests__` directories that it will find in your project structure. So, it's important to name your directories with `__tests__`.

Create a `TweetUtils-test.js` file inside `__tests__`:

```
jest.dontMock('../TweetUtils');

describe('Tweet utilities module', function () {

  it('returns an array of tweet ids', function () {

    var TweetUtils = require('../TweetUtils');
    var tweetsMock = {
      tweet1: {},
      tweet2: {},
      tweet3: {}
    };
    var expectedListOfTweetIds = [ 'tweet1', 'tweet2', 'tweet3' ];
    var actualListOfTweetIds = TweetUtils.
getListOfTweetIds(tweetsMock);

    expect(actualListOfTweetIds).toEqual(expectedListOfTweetIds);
  });
});
```

First, we tell Jest not to mock our `TweetUtils` module:

```
jest.dontMock('../TweetUtils');
```

We need to do this because Jest will *automatically* mock modules returned by the `require()` function. In our test, we require the `TweetUtils` module:

```
var TweetUtils = require('../TweetUtils');
```

Without the `jest.dontMock('../TweetUtils')` call, Jest would return an imitation of our `TweetUtils` module, instead of the real one. In this case, we actually need the real `TweetUtils` module because that's what we're testing.

Next, we call a global `describe()` Jest function. It's important to understand the concept behind it. In our `TweetUtils-test.js` file, we're not just creating a single test, instead we're creating a suit of tests. A suit is a collection of tests that collectively tests a bigger unit of functionality. For example, a suit can have multiple tests, which tests all the individual parts of a larger module. In our example, we have a `TweetUtils` module with potentially a number of utility functions. In this situation, we would create a suit for the `TweetUtils` module, and then create tests for each individual utility function, such as `getListOfTweetIds()`.

The `describe` function defines a suit and takes these two parameters:

- Suit name: This is the title that describes what is being tested by this `'Tweet utilities module'` suit
- Suit implementation: This is the function that implements this suit

In our example, the suit is as follows:

```
describe('Tweet utilities module', function () {
    // Suit implementation goes here...
});
```

How do you create an individual test? In Jest, individual tests are called **specs**. They are defined by calling another global `it()` Jest function. Just like `describe()`, the `it()` function takes two parameters:

- Spec name: This is the title that describes what is being tested by this `'returns an array of tweet ids'` spec
- Spec implementation: This is the function that implements this spec

In our example, the spec is as follows:

```
it('returns an array of tweet ids', function () {
    // Spec implementation goes here...
});
```

Let's take a closer look at the implementation of our spec:

```
var TweetUtils = require('../TweetUtils');
var tweetsMock = {
    tweet1: {},
    tweet2: {},
    tweet3: {}
};
var expectedListOfTweetIds = [ 'tweet1', 'tweet2', 'tweet3' ];
var actualListOfTweetIds = TweetUtils.getListOfTweetIds(tweetsMock);

expect(actualListOfTweetIds).toEqual(expectedListOfTweetIds);
```

This spec tests whether the `getListOfTweetIds()` method of our `TweetUtils` module returns an array of tweet IDs, when given an object with tweets.

First, we will import the `TweetUtils` module:

```
var TweetUtils = require('../TweetUtils');
```

Then, we will create a mock object that simulates the real tweets object:

```
var tweetsMock = {
  tweet1: {},
  tweet2: {},
  tweet3: {}
};
```

The only requirement for this mock object is to have tweet IDs as object keys. The values are not important, so we need to choose empty objects. The key names are not important as well, so we choose to name them tweet1, tweet2, and tweet3. This mock object doesn't fully simulate the real tweet object. Its sole purpose is to simulate the fact that its keys are tweet IDs.

The next step is to create an expected list of tweet IDs:

```
var expectedListOfTweetIds = [ 'tweet1', 'tweet2', 'tweet3' ];
```

We know what tweet IDs to expect because we've mocked the tweets object with the same IDs.

The next step is to extract the actual tweet IDs from our mocked tweets object. For this, we use the getListOfTweetIds() method that takes the tweets object and returns an array of tweet IDs:

```
var actualListOfTweetIds = TweetUtils.getListOfTweetIds(tweetsMock);
```

We pass the tweetsMock object to that method and store the results in the actualListOfTweetIds variable. The reason it's named actualListOfTweetIds is because this list of tweet IDs is produced by the actual getListOfTweetIds() function that we're testing.

The final step will introduce us to a new important concept:

```
expect(actualListOfTweetIds).toEqual(expectedListOfTweetIds);
```

Let's think about the process of testing. We need to take an actual value produced by the method that we're testing, that is, getListOfTweetIds(), and match it to the expected value that we know in advance. The result of that match will determine whether our test has passed or failed.

The reason why we can guess what getListOfTweetIds() will return in advance is because we've prepared the input for it; that's our mock object:

```
var tweetsMock = {
  tweet1: {},
  tweet2: {},
  tweet3: {}
};
```

So, we can expect the following output by calling `TweetUtils.getListOfTweetIds(tweetsMock)`:

```
[ 'tweet1', 'tweet2', 'tweet3' ]
```

Because something can go wrong inside `getListOfTweetIds()`, we cannot guarantee this result; we can only *expect* it.

That's why we need to create an expectation. In Jest, an **expectation** is built using the `expect()` function, which takes an actual value, for example, `actualListOfTweetIds` object: `expect(actualListOfTweetIds)`.

Then, we chain it with a **matcher** function that compares the actual value with the expected value and tells Jest whether the expectation was met or not:

```
expect(actualListOfTweetIds).toEqual(expectedListOfTweetIds);
```

In our example, we use the `toEqual()` matcher function to compare the two arrays. You can find a list of all the built-in matcher functions in Jest at `https://facebook.github.io/jest/docs/api.html#expect-value`.

This is how you create a spec. A spec contains one or more expectations. Each expectation tests the state of your code. A spec can be either a **passing spec** or a **failing spec**. A spec is a passing spec only when all the expectations are met, otherwise it's a failing spec.

Well done, you've written your first testing suit with a single spec that has one expectation. How can you run it?

Installing and running Jest

First, let's install the **Jest command-line interface (Jest CLI)**:

```
npm install --save-dev jest-cli
```

This command installs the Jest CLI, and adds it as a development dependency to our `~/snapterest/package.json` file. Next, let's edit the `package.json` file. We'll replace the existing `"script"` object:

```
"scripts": {
  "test": "echo \"Error: no test specified\" && exit 1"
},
```

Replace the preceding object with the following one:

```
"scripts": {
  "test": "jest"
},
```

Now we're ready to run our test suit. Navigate to the ~/snapterest/ directory, and run the following command:

```
npm test
```

You should see the following message in your Terminal:

```
Using Jest CLI v0.4.18
 PASS  source/utils/__tests__/TweetUtils-test.js (0.065s)
1 test passed (1 total)
Run time: 0.295s
```

As you can see, I am using Version 0.4.18 of the Jest CLI. When you run your test, the Jest version is likely to be higher than this.

The key line in this message is as follows:

```
PASS  source/utils/__tests__/TweetUtils-test.js (0.065s)
```

- PASS: This tells you that your test has passed
- source/utils/__tests__/TweetUtils-test.js: This tells you what test it was running
- (0.065s): This tells how long it took to run the test

That's all it takes to write and test a tiny unit test. Now, let's create another one!

Creating multiple specs and expectations

This time, we'll create and test the collection utility module. Create the CollectionUtils.js file in the ~/snapterest/source/utils/ directory:

```
function getNumberOfTweetsInCollection(collection) {
  var TweetUtils = require('./TweetUtils');
  var listOfCollectionTweetIds = TweetUtils.
getListOfTweetIds(collection);

  return listOfCollectionTweetIds.length;
}

function isEmptyCollection(collection) {
  return (getNumberOfTweetsInCollection(collection) === 0);
}
```

```
module.exports = {
  getNumberOfTweetsInCollection: getNumberOfTweetsInCollection,
  isEmptyCollection: isEmptyCollection
};
```

The `CollectionUtils` module has two methods:
`getNumberOfTweetsInCollection()` and `isEmptyCollection()`.

First, let's discuss `getNumberOfTweetsInCollection()`:

```
function getNumberOfTweetsInCollection(collection) {
  var TweetUtils = require('./TweetUtils');
  var listOfCollectionTweetIds = TweetUtils.
getListOfTweetIds(collection);

  return listOfCollectionTweetIds.length;
}
```

As you can see, this function requires the `TweetUtils` module as a dependency.
It then calls the `getListOfTweetIds()` method and passes the `collection`
object as a parameter. The result returned by `getListOfTweetIds()` is
stored in the `listOfCollectionTweetIds` variable, and since it's an array,
`getNumberOfTweetsInCollection()` returns a `length` property of that array.

Now, let's take a look at the `isEmptyCollection()` method:

```
function isEmptyCollection(collection) {
  return (getNumberOfTweetsInCollection(collection) === 0);
}
```

It reuses the `getNumberOfTweetsInCollection()` method that we just discussed. It
checks whether the result returned by a call to `getNumberOfTweetsInCollection()`
is equal to zero. Then, it returns the result of that check, which is either `true`
or `false`.

Finally, we export both the methods from this module:

```
module.exports = {
  getNumberOfTweetsInCollection: getNumberOfTweetsInCollection,
  isEmptyCollection: isEmptyCollection
};
```

We just created our `CollectionUtils` module. Our next task is to test it.

Inside the `~/snapterest/source/utils/__tests__/` directory, create the following `CollectionUtils-test.js` file:

```
jest.autoMockOff();

describe('Collection utilities module', function () {

  var CollectionUtils = require('../CollectionUtils');

  var collectionTweetsMock = {
    collectionTweet7: {},
    collectionTweet8: {},
    collectionTweet9: {}
  };

  it('returns a number of tweets in collection', function
getNumberOfTweetsInCollection() {

    var actualNumberOfTweetsInCollection = CollectionUtils.getNumberOf
TweetsInCollection(collectionTweetsMock);
    var expectedNumberOfTweetsInCollection = 3;

    expect(actualNumberOfTweetsInCollection).toBe(expectedNumberOfTwee
tsInCollection);

  });

  it('checks if collection is not empty', function
isNotEmptyCollection() {

    var actualIsEmptyCollectionValue = CollectionUtils.isEmptyCollecti
on(collectionTweetsMock);

    expect(actualIsEmptyCollectionValue).toBeDefined();
    expect(actualIsEmptyCollectionValue).toBe(false);
    expect(actualIsEmptyCollectionValue).not.toBe(true);

  });

});
```

The `CollectionUtils-test.js` is a bigger test suit than the one we created earlier. There are quite a few things to learn from it. Let's discuss it in detail.

The very first thing that we need to do is to tell Jest not to mock automatically:

```
jest.autoMockOff();
```

What does it mean to mock automatically? In the testing environment, Jest replaces your usual `require()` function with its own version. Jest's version of `require()` function loads the real module and replaces that module with its mock version. As a result, none of the `require()` function calls will work as expected in our testing environment. Not even the ones that are used to import the dependency modules inside a module that we're testing. This means that for the module that we want the test to work, we need to call `jest.dontMock()` for that module, and then for each module that it depends on. There can be a large number of dependency modules. So instead of calling `jest.dontMock()` too many times, we can reverse the situation by calling the `jest.autoMockOff()` method. Now Jest won't mock by default, which means that we will need to explicitly call the `jest.mock()` method for each module that we want to mock.

In `CollectionUtils-test.js`, we only import the two modules: `CollectionUtils` and its dependency module `TweetUtils`. So a less efficient alternative to `jest.autoMockOff()` would be as follows:

```
jest.dontMock('../CollectionUtils');
jest.dontMock('../TweetUtils');
```

Once you call `jest.autoMockOff()` to turn the automatic mocking off, you can then call `jest.autoMockOn()` to turn it back on later in your code.

After taking care of turning off the automatic mocking, we define our test suit:

```
describe('Collection utilities module', function () {

    var CollectionUtils = require('../CollectionUtils');

    var collectionTweetsMock = {
        collectionTweet7: {},
        collectionTweet8: {},
        collectionTweet9: {}
    };

    // Specs go here...
});
```

We give it a name `Collection utilities module`, since it describes exactly what module we're testing. Now let's take a look at the implementation of this test suit. Instead of immediately defining specs like we did in our previous test suit, we're importing the `CollectionUtils` module and creating the `collectionTweetsMock` object. So, are we allowed to do that? Absolutely. The test suite implementation function is just another JavaScript function, where we can do some work before we define our test specs.

This test suit will implement more than one spec. All of them will use the `collectionTweetsMock` object, so it makes sense to define it outside the specs' scope and reuse it inside the specs. As you might have already guessed, the `collectionTweetsMock` object imitates a collection of tweets.

Now let's implement the individual specs.

Our first spec tests whether the `CollectionUtils` module returns a number of tweets in the collection:

```
it('returns a number of tweets in collection', function
getNumberOfTweetsInCollection() {

  var actualNumberOfTweetsInCollection = CollectionUtils.getNumberOfTw
eetsInCollection(collectionTweetsMock);
  var expectedNumberOfTweetsInCollection = 3;

  expect(actualNumberOfTweetsInCollection).toBe(expectedNumberOfTweets
InCollection);

});
```

We first get the actual number of tweets in our mock collection:

```
var actualNumberOfTweetsInCollection = CollectionUtils.getNumberOfTwee
tsInCollection(collectionTweetsMock);
```

For this, we call the `getNumberOfTweetsInCollection()` method and pass the `collectionTweetsMock` object to it. Then, we define the number of expected tweets in our mock collection:

```
var expectedNumberOfTweetsInCollection = 3;
```

Finally, we call the `expect()` global function to create an expectation:

```
expect(actualNumberOfTweetsInCollection).toBe(expectedNumberOfTweetsI
nCollection);
```

We use the `toBe()` matcher function to match the actual value and the expected one.

If you now run the `npm test` command, you will see that both the test suits pass:

```
Using Jest CLI v0.4.18
 PASS   source/utils/__tests__/TweetUtils-test.js (0.094s)
 PASS   source/utils/__tests__/CollectionUtils-test.js (0.104s)
2 tests passed (2 total)
Run time: 1.297s
```

Remember that for a test suit to pass, it must have only the passing specs. For a spec to be passing, it must have all its expectations to be met. That's the case so far.

How about running a little evil experiment?

Open your `~/snapterest/source/utils/CollectionUtils.js` file, and inside the `getNumberOfTweetsInCollection()` function, go to the following line of code:

```
return listOfCollectionTweetIds.length;
```

Now change it to this:

```
return listOfCollectionTweetIds.length + 1;
```

What this tiny update will do is return an incorrect number of tweets in any given collection. Now run `npm test` one more time. You should see that all your specs in `CollectionUtils-test.js` have failed. Here is the one we're interested in:

```
FAIL   source/utils/__tests__/CollectionUtils-test.js (0.12s)
Collection utilities module > it returns a number of tweets in collection
  - Expected: 4 toBe: 3
        at Spec.getNumberOfTweetsInCollection (/Users/artemij/snapterest/
source/utils/__tests__/CollectionUtils-test.js:18:46)
        at Timer.listOnTimeout [as ontimeout] (timers.js:112:15)
. . .
```

We haven't seen a failing test before, so let's take a closer look at what it's trying to tell us.

First, it gives us the bad news that the `CollectionUtils-test.js` test has failed:

```
FAIL   source/utils/__tests__/CollectionUtils-test.js (0.12s)
```

Then, it tells us in a human-friendly manner what we were testing:

```
Collection utilities module > it returns a number of tweets in collection
```

Then, what went wrong; the unexpected test result:

```
- Expected: 4 toBe: 3
```

Finally, Jest prints a stack trace that should give us enough technical details to quickly identify what part of our code has produced the unexpected result:

```
at Spec.getNumberOfTweetsInCollection (/Users/artemij/snapterest/source/
utils/__tests__/CollectionUtils-test.js:18:46)
at Timer.listOnTimeout [as ontimeout] (timers.js:112:15)
```

Notice that it says at which spec an expectation wasn't met:

```
at Spec.getNumberOfTweetsInCollection
```

The `getNumberOfTweetsInCollection` function is the name of the function that implements that spec:

```
it('returns a number of tweets in collection', function
getNumberOfTweetsInCollection() {

    // Spec implementation goes here...

});
```

Choosing to name the function that implements your spec proves to be very helpful in the case where it fails.

Alright! Enough of failing our tests on purpose. Let's revert our `~/snapterest/source/utils/CollectionUtils.js` file as follows:

```
return listOfCollectionTweetIds.length;
```

The distinct difference between our previous test suit and `CollectionUtils-test.js` is the number of specs. A test suit in Jest can have many specs that test different methods of a single module.

Our `CollectionUtils` module has two methods. Our test suit for it will have three specs. Let's discuss the other two.

Our next spec in `CollectionUtils-test.js` checks whether the collection is not empty:

```
it('checks if collection is not empty', function
isNotEmptyCollection() {

    var actualIsEmptyCollectionValue = CollectionUtils.isEmptyCollection
(collectionTweetsMock);
```

```
expect(actualIsEmptyCollectionValue).toBeDefined();
expect(actualIsEmptyCollectionValue).toBe(false);
expect(actualIsEmptyCollectionValue).not.toBe(true);

});
```

First, we call the `isEmptyCollection()` method and pass the `collectionTweetsMock` object to it. We store the result in the `actualIsEmptyCollectionValue` variable. Notice how we're reusing the same `collectionTweetsMock` object, as in our previous spec.

Next, we create not one but three expectations:

```
expect(actualIsEmptyCollectionValue).toBeDefined();
expect(actualIsEmptyCollectionValue).toBe(false);
expect(actualIsEmptyCollectionValue).not.toBe(true);
```

You might have already guessed what we're expecting from our `actualIsEmptyCollectionValue`:

We expect it to be defined as follows:

```
expect(actualIsEmptyCollectionValue).toBeDefined();
```

This means that the `isEmptyCollection()` function must return something other than `undefined`.

We expect its value to be `false`:

```
expect(actualIsEmptyCollectionValue).toBe(false);
```

Earlier, we used the `toEqual()` matcher function to compare the arrays. `toEqual()` does a deep comparison, which is perfect for comparing arrays, but it is an overkill for primitive values, such as `false`.

Finally, we expect `actualIsEmptyCollectionValue` not to be `true`:

```
expect(actualIsEmptyCollectionValue).not.toBe(true);
```

The `.not` inverses the next comparison. It matches the expectation with the inverse of `toBe(true)` with `false`.

Notice that `toBe(false)` and `not.toBe(true)` produce the same result.

Only when all the three expectations are met, then this spec is passing.

So far, we've tested the utility modules, but how do you test the React components with Jest? Let's find this out next.

Testing React components

Just like with utility modules, creating tests for React components starts with creating the __tests__ directory. Navigate to ~/snapterest/source/components/ and create the __tests__ directory.

The first React component that we'll test will be our Header component. Create Header-test.js in the ~/snapterest/source/components/__tests__ directory:

```
jest.dontMock('../Header.react');

describe('Header component', function () {

  it('renders provided header text', function () {

    var React = require('react');
    var ReactDOM = require('react-dom');
    var TestUtils = require('react-addons-test-utils');
    var Header = require('../Header.react');

    var header = TestUtils.renderIntoDocument(
      <Header text="Testing..." />
    );

    var actualHeaderText = ReactDOM.findDOMNode(header).textContent;

    expect(actualHeaderText).toBe('Testing...');

    var defaultHeader = TestUtils.renderIntoDocument(
      <Header />
    );

    var actualDefaultHeaderText = ReactDOM.findDOMNode(defaultHeader).
  textContent;

    expect(actualDefaultHeaderText).toBe('Default header');
  });
});
```

By now, you can recognize the structure of our test files. First, we tell Jest not to mock the Header component. Then, we define our test suit, and we give it a name, 'Header component'. Our test suit has one spec named, renders provided header text. As the name suggests, it tests whether our Header component renders the provided header text. The implementation of that spec has a number of new things that we'll discuss. Let's take a closer look at them.

First, we import React and ReactDOM:

```
var React = require('react');
var ReactDOM = require('react-dom');
```

Then, we import one of the React add-ons:

```
var TestUtils = require('react-addons-test-utils');
```

`TestUtils` helps you test the React components with any test framework that you choose. Naturally, it works great with Jest. Let's install it:

npm install --save-dev react-addons-test-utils

Next, in order to test our `Header` component, we need to import it:

```
var Header = require('../Header.react');
```

Our next task is to render the `Header` component to the DOM. The `TestUtils` add-on has a helper `renderIntoDocument()` function that does exactly this:

```
var header = TestUtils.renderIntoDocument(
  <Header text="Testing..." />
);
```

We pass the React `<Header text="Testing..." />` component instance to the `renderIntoDocument()` function as a parameter. Notice that in this case, our `Header` component instance has a `text` property. `renderIntoDocument()` returns a reference to that component.

Now, we have a reference to our `Header` component that is rendered to the DOM. Our next task is to check what header text did it render. This means that we need to perform the following steps:

1. Find the component's DOM node.
2. Get the DOM node's text content.

Do you remember what method React provides us to find the component's DOM node? Did you say `ReactDOM.findDOMNode()`?

```
ReactDOM.findDOMNode(header)
```

We pass `header` to `ReactDOM.findDOMNode()` as a parameter. As a result, `ReactDOM.findDOMNode()` returns a DOM node element. Now we can access its `textContent` property:

```
ReactDOM.findDOMNode(header).textContent;
```

The value of the `textContent` property becomes the actual header text:

```
var actualHeaderText = ReactDOM.findDOMNode(header).textContent;
```

The final step is to create an expectation and match it with the expected text:

```
expect(actualHeaderText).toBe('Testing...');
```

As you can tell, we're expecting `Testing...` to be rendered as a DOM node text.

Great! Now we can test that the provided header text to the `Header` component instance is rendered to the DOM.

What happens when we create the `Header` component instance without providing any header text?

Let's find this out by rendering another instance of the `Header` component to the DOM:

```
var defaultHeader = TestUtils.renderIntoDocument(
  <Header />
);
```

Only this time, it has no `text` property. We'll call this component reference `defaultHeader`. Let's find the `defaultHeader` component's DOM node element and access its `textContent` property:

```
var actualDefaultHeaderText = ReactDOM.findDOMNode(defaultHeader).
textContent;
```

This will be our actual header text rendered by default by a `Header` component. Finally, we create an expectation and match this with the expected text:

```
expect(actualDefaultHeaderText).toBe('Default header');
```

In this case, `actualDefaultHeaderText` must be equal to `Default header`.

This is how you test what your React component renders. You might be wondering how do you test the behavior of your React component?

That's what we'll discuss next!

Create the `Button-test.js` file in the `~/snapterest/source/components/__tests__/` directory:

```
jest.dontMock('../Button.react');

describe('Button component', function () {
```

```
it('calls handler function on click', function () {

  var React = require('react');
  var TestUtils = require('react-addons-test-utils');
  var Button = require('../Button.react');
  var handleClick = jest.genMockFunction();

  var button = TestUtils.renderIntoDocument(
    <Button handleClick={handleClick} />
  );

  var buttonInstance = TestUtils.findRenderedDOMComponentWithTag(but
ton, 'button');

  TestUtils.Simulate.click(buttonInstance);

  expect(handleClick).toBeCalled();

  var numberOfCallsMadeIntoMockFunction = handleClick.mock.calls.
length;

  expect(numberOfCallsMadeIntoMockFunction).toBe(1);
  });
});
```

The `Button-test.js` file will test our `Button` component, and specifically, check whether it triggers the event handler function when you click on it. Without further ado, let's focus on the `'calls handler function on click'` spec implementation:

```
var React = require('react/addons');
var TestUtils = require('react-addons-test-utils');
var Button = require('../Button.react');
var handleClick = jest.genMockFunction();

var button = TestUtils.renderIntoDocument(
  <Button handleClick={handleClick} />
);

var buttonInstance = TestUtils.findRenderedDOMComponentWithTag(button,
'button');

TestUtils.Simulate.click(buttonInstance);
```

```
expect(handleClick).toBeCalled();

var numberOfCallsMadeIntoMockFunction = handleClick.mock.calls.length;

expect(numberOfCallsMadeIntoMockFunction).toBe(1);
```

First, we're importing React with the add-ons module and our `Button` component. As usual, we tell Jest not to mock the `Button` component.

Before we continue with implementing our spec, let's talk about how we're going to implement it. The plan is to:

1. Generate a mock function.
2. Render the `Button` component instance with our mock function that imitates a click handler.
3. Find the instance of our rendered `Button` component.
4. Simulate a click event on that component instance.
5. Check whether a click event handler function was triggered.
6. Check whether our mock function was called exactly once.

Let's generate a mock function:

```
var handleClick = jest.genMockFunction();
```

The `jest.genMockFunction()` function returns the newly generated Jest mock function ; we name it `handleClick`.

Next, we render the instance of our `Button` component to the DOM:

```
var button = TestUtils.renderIntoDocument(
  <Button handleClick={handleClick} />
);
```

This `Button` component instance receives our mock `handleClick` function as a property.

Then, we find the `Button` component instance rendered to the DOM:

```
var buttonInstance = TestUtils.findRenderedDOMComponentWithTag(button,
  'button');
```

The `TestUtils.findRenderedDOMComponentWithTag()` method finds one instance of the `Button` component that is rendered as a `button` tag. We store that instance in the `buttonInstance` variable.

Next, we simulate a click on that component instance:

```
TestUtils.Simulate.click(buttonInstance);
```

`TestUtils.Simulate` simulates an event dispatch on a DOM node. For our purposes, we need to simulate a click event dispatch. For this, we need to call the `TestUtils.Simulate.click()` method and pass `buttonInstance` as a DOM node element. `TestUtils.Simulate` provides an event method such as `click()` for all events supported by React.

Finally, we create an expectation:

```
expect(handleClick).toBeCalled();
```

As you might have guessed, we expect our `handleClick` mock function to be called at least once during our test.

What we also want to check is whether it's called exactly once. How do we check the number of calls made into our `handleClick` mock function? All the Jest mock functions have a special `.mock` property that stores all the data about how the mock function was called. We'll take a look at our `handleClick` mock function's `.mock` property to find out how many times `handleClick` was called:

```
var numberOfCallsMadeIntoMockFunction = handleClick.mock.calls.length;
```

The `.mock` property has the `.calls` property, which is an array, that represents all the calls that have been made into our `handleClick` mock function. The length of that array will be the number of calls made into `handleClick`. We store this number in the `numberOfCallsMadeIntoMockFunction` variable and then create another expectation:

```
expect(numberOfCallsMadeIntoMockFunction).toBe(1);
```

We expect the number of calls made into our mock function to be exactly 1.

Right now, we've finished creating our tests. However, we can't run them yet; can you guess why? Let's think about it. We're testing the React components written in the JSX syntax, but Jest doesn't understand the JSX syntax. So, if you run `npm test` now, both the component tests will fail and report `SyntaxError`.

What we need to do is to configure Jest in order to use a preprocessor provided by the `babel-jest` module. Add the `jest` property to your `~/snapterest/package.json` file:

```
"jest": {
  "scriptPreprocessor": "<rootDir>/node_modules/babel-jest",
  "testFileExtensions": ["es6", "js"],
  "unmockedModulePathPatterns": [
```

```
        "<rootDir>/node_modules/react"
    ]
  }
}
```

Install `babel-jest`:

npm install --save-dev babel-jest

If you're curious about what `unmockedModulePathPatterns` does, then go to `https://facebook.github.io/jest/docs/api.html#config-unmockedmodulepathpatterns-array-string`.

Now it's time to run all our tests.

Navigate to `~/snapterest/` and run this command:

npm test

All your test suits should PASS:

PASS source/utils/__tests__/TweetUtils-test.js (0.134s)

PASS source/utils/__tests__/CollectionUtils-test.js (0.146s)

PASS source/components/__tests__/Button-test.js (2.802s)

PASS source/components/__tests__/Header-test.js (2.877s)

4 tests passed (4 total)

Run time: 4.728s

Log messages, such as these, will help you sleep well at night and go on holidays, without the need to constantly check your work e-mails.

Summary

Now you know how to create the React components and unit test them.

In this chapter, you learned the essentials of Jest; the unit testing framework from Facebook that works well with React. We discussed the test suits, specs, expectations, and matchers. We created mocks and simulated click events.

In the next chapter, we'll learn the essentials of the Flux architecture, and how to improve the maintainability of our React application.

9
Supercharge Your React Architecture with Flux

The process of building a web application has one quality that somewhat mirrors the process of evolution of life itself; it never ends. Unlike building a bridge, building a web application has no natural state that represents the end of the development process. It's up to you or your team to decide when you should stop the development process and release what you've already built.

In this book, we reached that point at which we can stop developing Snapterest. Right now, we have a small React.js application with a basic functionality that simply works.

Isn't that enough?

Not exactly. Earlier in this book, we discussed how the process of maintaining your web application is much more expensive in terms of time and effort than the process of developing it. If we choose to finish developing Snapterest at its current state, we'll also choose to start the process of maintaining it.

Are we ready for maintaining Snapterest? Do we know if its current state will allow us to introduce a new functionality later on without any significant code refactoring?

Analyzing your web application's architecture

To answer these questions, let's zoom away from the implementation details and explore our application's architecture:

- The `app.js` file renders our `Application` component
- The `Application` component manages a collection of tweets and renders our `Stream` and `Collection` components
- The `Stream` component receives the new tweets from the `SnapkiteStreamClient` library and renders the `StreamTweet` and `Header` components
- The `Collection` component renders the `CollectionControls` and `TweetList` components

Stop right there. Can you tell how data flows inside our application? Do you know where it enters our application? How does a new tweet end up in our collection? Let's examine our data flow more closely:

1. We use the `SnapkiteStreamClient` library to receive a new tweet inside a `Stream` component.
2. This new tweet is then passed from `Stream` to the `StreamTweet` component.
3. The `StreamTweet` component passes it to the `Tweet` component, which renders the tweet image.
4. A user clicks on that tweet image to add it to its collection.
5. The `Tweet` component passes the `tweet` object to the `StreamTweet` component via the `handleImageClick(tweet)` callback function.
6. The `StreamTweet` component passes that `tweet` object to the `Stream` component via the `onAddTweetToCollection(tweet)` callback function.
7. The `Stream` component passes that `tweet` object to the `Application` component via the `onAddTweetToCollection(tweet)` callback function.
8. The `Application` component adds `tweet` to the `collectionTweets` object and updates its state.
9. The state update triggers the `Application` component to re-render, which in turn re-renders the `Collection` component with an updated collection of tweets.
10. Then, the child components of the `Collection` component can mutate our collection of tweets as well.

Do you feel already confused? Can you rely on this architecture in the long run? Do you think it's easily maintainable? I don't think so.

Let's identify the key problems with our current architecture. We can see that the new data enters our React application via the `Stream` component. It then travels all the way down to the `Tweet` component in the component hierarchy. Then, it travels all the way up to the `Application` component, where it's stored and managed.

Why do we store and manage our collection tweets in the `Application` component? Because `Application` is a parent component for two other components: `Stream` and `Collection`. Both of them need to be able to mutate our collection tweets. In order to accommodate this, our `Application` component needs to pass callback functions to both the components:

- The Stream component:

  ```
  <Stream onAddTweetToCollection={this.addTweetToCollection} />
  ```

- The Collection component:

  ```
  <Collection
    tweets={this.state.collectionTweets}
    onRemoveTweetFromCollection={this.removeTweetFromCollection}
    onRemoveAllTweetsFromCollection={this.
  removeAllTweetsFromCollection} />
  ```

The `Stream` component gets the `onAddTweetToCollection()` function to add a tweet to the collection. The `Collection` component gets the `onRemoveTweetFromCollection()` function to remove a tweet from the collection, and the `onRemoveAllTweetsFromCollection()` function to remove all the tweets from the collection.

These callback functions are then propagated down to the component hierarchy until they reach some component that actually calls them. In our application, the `onAddTweetToCollection()` function is only called in the `Tweet` component. Let's take a look at how many times it needs to be passed from one component to another before it can be called in a `Tweet` component:

```
Application > Stream > StreamTweet > Tweet
```

`onAddTweetToCollection()` is not used in the `Stream` and `StreamTweet` components, yet both of them get it as a property for the purpose of passing it down to their child components.

Snapterest is a small React application, so this problem is rather an inconvenience, but later on, if you decide to add new features, this inconvenience will quickly become a maintenance nightmare:

```
Application > ComponentA > ComponentB > ComponentC > ComponentD >
ComponentE > ComponentF > ComponentG > Tweet
```

To prevent this from happening, we're going to solve two problems:

- We'll change how the new data enters our application
- We'll change how the components get and set data

We'll rethink of how data flows inside our application with the help of Flux.

Understanding Flux

Flux is the application architecture from Facebook that complements React. It's not a framework or a library, but rather a solution to a common problem; how to build scalable client-side applications.

With the Flux architecture, we can rethink how data flows inside our application. Flux makes sure that all our data flows only in a **single direction**. This helps us reason about how our application works, regardless of how small or large it is. With Flux, we can add a new functionality without exploding our application's complexity.

You might have noticed that both React and Flux share the same core concept; one-way data flow. That's why they naturally work well together. We know how data flows inside a React component, but how does Flux implement the one-way data flow?

With Flux, we separate the concerns of our application into four logical entities:

- Actions
- Dispatcher
- Stores
- Views

Actions are objects that we create when our application's state changes. For example, when our application receives a new tweet, we create a new action. An action object has a `type` property that identifies what action it is and any other properties that our application needs to transition to a new state. Here is an example of an action object:

```
var action = {
  type: 'receive_tweet',
  tweet: tweet
};
```

As you can see, this is an action of type `receive_tweet`, and it has the `tweet` property, which is a new tweet object that our application has received. You can guess in which case this action is created by looking at its type. For each new tweet that our application receives, it creates a `receive_tweet` action.

Where does this action go? What part of our application gets this action? Actions are dispatched to stores.

Stores are responsible for managing your application's data. They provide methods for accessing that data, but not for changing it. If you want to change data in stores, you have to create and dispatch an action.

We know how to create an action, but how do you dispatch it? As the name suggests, you can use a dispatcher for this.

The dispatcher is responsible for dispatching all the actions to all stores:

- It stores register with a dispatcher. They provide a callback function.
- All actions are dispatched by a dispatcher to all the stores that are registered with it.

This is how our data flow looks like:

```
Actions > Dispatcher > Stores
```

You can see that the dispatcher plays a role of a central element in our data flow. All actions are dispatched by it. Stores register with it. All the actions are dispatched synchronously. You can't dispatch an action in the middle of the previous action dispatch. No action can skip the dispatcher in the Flux architecture.

Creating a dispatcher

Now let's implement this data flow. We'll start by creating a dispatcher first. Facebook offers us its implementation of a dispatcher that we can reuse. Let's take advantage of this.

1. Navigate to the ~/snapterest directory and run the following command:

   ```
   npm install --save flux
   ```

   The flux module comes with a Dispatcher function that we'll be reusing.

2. Next, create a new folder called dispatcher in our project's ~/snapterest/source/dispatcher directory. Now create the AppDispatcher.js file in it:

   ```
   var Dispatcher = require('flux').Dispatcher;
   module.exports = new Dispatcher();
   ```

First, we import Dispatcher provided by Facebook, then create, and export a new instance of it. Now we can use this instance in our application.

Next, we need a convenient way of creating and dispatching actions. For each action, let's create a function that creates and dispatches that action. These functions will be our action creators.

Creating an action creator

Let's create a new folder called actions in our project's ~/snapterest/source/actions directory. Then, create the TweetActionCreators.js file in it:

```
var AppDispatcher = require('../dispatcher/AppDispatcher');

function receiveTweet(tweet) {

  var action = {
    type: 'receive_tweet',
    tweet: tweet
  };

  AppDispatcher.dispatch(action);
}

module.exports = {
  receiveTweet: receiveTweet
};
```

Our action creators will need a dispatcher to dispatch the actions. We will import `AppDispatcher` that we created previously:

```
var AppDispatcher = require('../dispatcher/AppDispatcher');
```

Then, we create our first action creator `receiveTweet()`:

```
function receiveTweet(tweet) {

  var action = {
    type: 'receive_tweet',
    tweet: tweet
  };

  AppDispatcher.dispatch(action);
}
```

The `receiveTweet()` function takes the `tweet` object as an argument, and creates the `action` object with a `type` property set to `receive_tweet`. It also adds the `tweet` object to our `action` object, and now every store will receive this `tweet` object.

Finally, the `receiveTweet()` action creator dispatches our `action` object by calling the `dispatch()` method on the `AppDispatcher` object:

```
AppDispatcher.dispatch(action);
```

The `dispatch()` method dispatches the `action` object to all the stores registered with the `AppDispatcher` dispatcher.

So far, we've created `AppDispatcher` and `TweetActionCreators`. Next, let's create our first store.

Creating a store

As we learned earlier, stores manage data in your Flux architecture. They provide that data to the React components. We're going to create a simple store that manages a new tweet that our application receives from Twitter.

Create new folder called `stores` in our project's `~/snapterest/source/stores` directory. Then, create the `TweetStore.js` file in it:

```
var AppDispatcher = require('../dispatcher/AppDispatcher');
var EventEmitter = require('events').EventEmitter;
var assign = require('object-assign');
```

```javascript
var tweet = null;

function setTweet(receivedTweet) {
  tweet = receivedTweet;
}

function emitChange() {
  TweetStore.emit('change');
}

var TweetStore = assign({}, EventEmitter.prototype, {

  addChangeListener: function (callback) {
    this.on('change', callback);
  },

  removeChangeListener: function (callback) {
    this.removeListener('change', callback);
  },

  getTweet: function () {
    return tweet;
  }

});

function handleAction(action) {
  if (action.type === 'receive_tweet') {
    setTweet(action.tweet);
    emitChange();
  }
}

TweetStore.dispatchToken = AppDispatcher.register(handleAction);

module.exports = TweetStore;
```

The `TweetStore.js` file implements a simple store. We can break it into four logical parts:

- Importing dependency modules and creating private data and methods
- Creating the `TweetStore` object with public methods
- Creating an action handler and registering a store with a dispatcher
- Assigning `dispatchToken` to our `TweetStore` object and exporting it

In the first logical part of our store, we're simply importing the dependency modules that our store needs:

```
var AppDispatcher = require('../dispatcher/AppDispatcher');
var EventEmitter = require('events').EventEmitter;
var assign = require('object-assign');
```

Because our store will need to register with a dispatcher, we import the `AppDispatcher` module. Next, we import the `EventEmitter` class to be able to add and remove event listeners from our store:

```
var EventEmitter = require('events').EventEmitter;
```

Finally, we import the `object-assign` module that copies the properties from multiple source objects to a single target object:

```
var assign = require('object-assign');
```

Let's install this module:

npm install --save object-assign

Once we import all the dependencies, we then define the data that our store manages:

```
var tweet = null;
```

`TweetStore` manages a simple tweet object that we initially set to `null` to identify that we didn't receive the new tweet yet.

Next, let's create the two private methods:

```
function setTweet(receivedTweet) {
  tweet = receivedTweet;
}

function emitChange() {
  TweetStore.emit('change');
}
```

The `setTweet()` function updates `tweet` with a `receiveTweet` object. The `emitChange` function emits the `change` event on the `TweetStore` object. These methods are private to the `TweetStore` module and not accessible outside it.

The second logical part of the `TweetStore.js` file is creating the `TweetStore` object:

```
var TweetStore = assign({}, EventEmitter.prototype, {

  addChangeListener: function (callback) {
    this.on('change', callback);
  },

  removeChangeListener: function (callback) {
    this.removeListener('change', callback);
  },

  getTweet: function () {
    return tweet;
  }

});
```

We want our store to be able to notify other parts of our application when it changes its data. We'll use events for this. Whenever our store updates its data, it emits the change event. Anyone interested in data changes can listen to this change event. They need to add their event listener function that our store will trigger on every change event. For this, our store defines the `addChangeListener()` method that adds the event listener, which listens to the change event, and the `removeChangeListener()` method that removes the change event listener. However, `addChangeListener()` and `removeChangeListener()` depend on methods provided by the `EventEmitter.prototype` object. So we need to copy the methods from the `EventEmitter.prototype` object to our `TweetStore` object. That's what the `assign()` function does:

```
targetObject = assign(targetObject, sourceObject1, sourceObject2);
```

It copies the properties owned by `sourceObject1` and `sourceObject2` to `targetObject` and then it returns `targetObject`. In our case, `sourceObject1` is `EventEmitter.prototype`, and `sourceObject2` is an object literal that defines our store's methods:

```
{

  addChangeListener: function (callback) {
    this.on('change', callback);
  },

  removeChangeListener: function (callback) {
    this.removeListener('change', callback);
  },

  getTweet: function () {
```

```
        return tweet;
    }

  }
```

`assign()` returns `targetObject` with the properties copied from all the source objects. That's what our `TweetStore` object is.

Have you noticed that we define the `getTweet()` function as a method of our `TweetStore` object, whereas we don't do that with the `setTweet()` function. Why is that?

Later on, we'll export the `TweetStore` object, which means that all its properties will be available for other parts of our application to use. We want them to be able to get the data from `TweetStore`, but not update that data directly by calling `setTweet()`. Instead, the only way to update data in any store is to create an action and dispatch it using a dispatcher to stores that has registered with that dispatcher. When the store gets that action, it can decide how to update its data.

This is a very important aspect of the Flux architecture. Stores are in full control of managing their data. They only allow other parts in our application to read that data, but never write to it directly. Only actions should mutate data in the stores.

The third logical part of the `TweetStore.js` file is creating an action handler and registering the store with a dispatcher.

First, we create the action handler function:

```
function handleAction(action) {
  if (action.type === 'receive_tweet') {
    setTweet(action.tweet);
    emitChange();
  }
}
```

The `handleAction()` function takes an `action` object as a parameter and checks its type property. In Flux, all stores get all the actions, but not all stores are interested in all the actions, so each store must decide what actions it's interested in. For this, a store must check for the action type. In our `TweetStore` store, we check whether the action type is `receive_tweet`, which means that our application has received a new tweet. If that's the case, then our `TweetStore` calls its private `setTweet()` function to update the `tweet` object with a new one that comes from the `action` object, that is, `action.tweet`. When the store changes its data, it needs to tell everyone who is interested in the data change. For this, it calls its private `emitChange()` function that emits the `change` event and triggers all the event listeners created by other parts in our application.

Our next task is to register the `TweetStore` store with a dispatcher. To register a store with a dispatcher, you need to call a dispatcher's `register()` method and pass the store's action handler function to it as a callback function. Whenever the dispatcher dispatches an action, it calls that callback function and passes the action object to it.

Let's take a look at our example:

```
TweetStore.dispatchToken = AppDispatcher.register(handleAction);
```

We call the `register()` method of `AppDispatcher`, and we pass the `handleAction` function to that method. The `register()` method returns a token that identifies `TweetStore`, and we can use it in other methods of `AppDispatcher`. We also save that token as a property of our `TweetStore` object.

The fourth logical part of the `TweetStore.js` file is exporting the `TweetStore` object:

```
module.exports = TweetStore;
```

That's how you create a simple store. Now, when we have implemented our first action creator, dispatcher, and store, let's revisit the Flux architecture and take a look at a bigger picture of how it works:

1. The stores register themselves with a dispatcher.
2. Action creators create and dispatch actions to the stores via a dispatcher.
3. Stores check for relevant actions and change their data accordingly.
4. Stores notify everyone who is listening about the data change.

Well that makes sense, you may say, but what triggers action creators? Who is listening to store updates? These are very good questions to ask. And the answers are awaiting you in our next chapter.

Summary

In this chapter, we analyzed our React application's architecture. We learned about the core concepts behind the Flux architecture, and implemented a dispatcher, action creator, and a store. In the next chapter, we'll integrate them into our React application and get its architecture ready for a maintenance paradise.

10
Prepare Your React Application for Painless Maintenance with Flux

The reason why we decided to implement the Flux architecture in our React application is that we wanted to have a data flow that is easier to maintain. In the previous chapter, we implemented `AppDispatcher`, `TweetActionCreators`, and `TweetStore`. Let's quickly re-cap what they are used for:

- `TweetActionCreators` creates and dispatches the actions
- `AppDispatcher` dispatches all the actions to all stores
- `TweetStore` stores and manages the application data

The only missing parts in our data flow are bits of functionality that are as follows:

- Use `TweetActionCreators` to create the actions and start the data flowing
- Use `TweetStore` to get data

Here are some important questions to ask: Where in our application does the data flow start? What is our data? If we answer these questions, we will understand where to start refactoring our application to adapt to the Flux architecture.

Snapterest allows users to receive and collect the latest tweets. The only data that our application is concerned with is tweets, so our data flow begins with receiving the new tweets. At the moment, what part of our application is responsible for receiving the new tweets? You might remember that our `Stream` component has the following `componentDidMount()` method:

```
componentDidMount: function () {
    SnapkiteStreamClient.initializeStream(this.handleNewTweet);
}
```

Yes, currently, we initiate a stream of new tweets after we render the `Stream` component. "Wait," you might say, "didn't we learn that React components should only be concerned with rendering the user interface?" You're correct. Unfortunately, at the moment, the `Stream` component is responsible for two different things:

- Rendering the `StreamTweet` component
- Initiating the data flow

Clearly, it will be a potential maintenance issue the in future. Let's decouple these two different concerns with the help of Flux.

Decoupling concerns with Flux

First, we'll create a new utility module called `WebAPIUtils`. Create `WebAPIUtils.js` in the `~/snapterest/source/utils/` directory:

```
var SnapkiteStreamClient = require('snapkite-stream-client');
var TweetActionCreators = require('../actions/TweetActionCreators');

function initializeStreamOfTweets() {    SnapkiteStreamClient.initiali
zeStream(TweetActionCreators.receiveTweet);
}

module.exports = {
    initializeStreamOfTweets: initializeStreamOfTweets
};
```

In this utility module, we first import the `SnapkiteStreamClient` library and `TweetActionCreators`. Then, we create the `initializeStreamOfTweets()` function that initializes a stream of new tweets, just like in the `componentDidMount()` method of the `Stream` component, except with one key difference: whenever `SnapkiteStreamClient` receives a new tweet, it calls the `TweetActionCreators.receiveTweet` method that passes a new tweet to it as an argument:

```
SnapkiteStreamClient.initializeStream(TweetActionCreators.
receiveTweet);
```

Remember that the `TweetActionCreators.receiveTweet` function expects to receive a `tweet` argument:

```
function receiveTweet(tweet) {
  // ... create and dispatch 'receive_tweet' action
}
```

This tweet will then be dispatched as a property of a new action object that the `receiveTweet()` function creates.

Then, the `WebAPIUtils` module exports our `initializeStreamOfTweets()` method:

```
module.exports = {
  initializeStreamOfTweets: initializeStreamOfTweets
};
```

Now we have a module with a method that initiates the data flow in our Flux architecture. Where should we import and call it? Since it's decoupled from the `Stream` component, and in fact, it doesn't depend on any React component at all, we can use it even before React renders anything. Let's use it in our `app.js` file:

```
var React = require('react');
var ReactDOM = require('react-dom');
var Application = require('./components/Application.react');
var WebAPIUtils = require('./utils/WebAPIUtils');

WebAPIUtils.initializeStreamOfTweets();

ReactDOM.render(<Application />, document.getElementById('react-application'));
```

As you can see, all that we need to do is import it and call the `initializeStreamOfTweets()` method:

```
var WebAPIUtils = require('./utils/WebAPIUtils');

WebAPIUtils.initializeStreamOfTweets();
```

We do this before calling React's `render()` method:

```
ReactDOM.render(<Application />, document.getElementById('react-application'));
```

In fact, for the purpose of experimentation, you can remove the `ReactDOM.render()` line of code altogether and put a log statement in the `TweetActionCreators.` `receiveTweet` function. For example, run the following code:

```
function receiveTweet(tweet) {

    console.log("I've received a new tweet and now will dispatch it
together with a new action.");

    var action = {
      type: 'receive_tweet',
      tweet: tweet
    };

    AppDispatcher.dispatch(action);
}
```

Don't forget to run the `gulp` command. Then, in your web browser, you will see the following output:

I am about to learn the essentials of React.js.

While on your web browser's console, you will see this output:

```
[Snapkite Stream Client] Socket connected
I've received a new tweet and now will dispatch it together with a new
action.
```

This log message will be printed out for each new tweet that our application receives. Even though we didn't render any React component, our Flux architecture is still there:

1. Our application receives a new tweet.
2. It creates and dispatches a new action.
3. No stores have registered with the dispatcher, so there is no one to receive the new action; hence, nothing is happening.

Now you can clearly see how React and Flux are two separate things that don't depend on each other at all.

We do want to render our React components. After all, we've put so much effort into creating them over the course of the last nine chapters! For this, we need to put our `TweetStore` into action. Can you tell where should we use it? We should use it in a React component that needs a tweet to render itself; our good old `Stream` component.

Refactoring the Stream component

Now, with the Flux architecture in place, we will rethink how our React components get the data that they need to render. As you know, there are usually two sources of data for a React component:

- Calling another library; for example, in our case, calling the `jQuery.ajax()` method or `SnapkiteStreamClient.initializeStream()`
- Receiving data from a parent React component via the `props` object

We want our React components not to use any external libraries to receive data. Instead, from now on, they will get that same data from stores. Keeping this plan in mind, let's refactor our `Stream` component.

Here is how it looks now:

```
var React = require('react');
var SnapkiteStreamClient = require('snapkite-stream-client');
var StreamTweet = require('./StreamTweet.react');
var Header = require('./Header.react');

var Stream = React.createClass({

  getInitialState: function () {
    return {
      tweet: null
    }
  },

  componentDidMount: function () {
    SnapkiteStreamClient.initializeStream(this.handleNewTweet);
  },

  componentWillUnmount: function () {
    SnapkiteStreamClient.destroyStream();
  },

  handleNewTweet: function (tweet) {
    this.setState({
      tweet: tweet
    });
  },
```

```
  render: function () {
    var tweet = this.state.tweet;

    if (tweet) {
      return (
        <StreamTweet
        tweet={tweet}
        onAddTweetToCollection={this.props.onAddTweetToCollection} />
      );
    }

    return (
      <Header text="Waiting for public photos from Twitter..." />
    );
  }
});
```

```
module.exports = Stream;
```

First, let's get rid of the `componentDidMount()`, `componentWillUnmount()`, and `handleNewTweet()` methods, and import the `TweetStore` store:

```
var React = require('react');
var StreamTweet = require('./StreamTweet.react');
var Header = require('./Header.react');
var TweetStore = require('../stores/TweetStore');

var Stream = React.createClass({

  getInitialState: function () {
    return {
      tweet: null
    }
  },

  render: function () {
    var tweet = this.state.tweet;

    if (tweet) {
      return (
        <StreamTweet
        tweet={tweet}
        onAddTweetToCollection={this.props.onAddTweetToCollection} />
```

```
      );
    }

    return (
      <Header text="Waiting for public photos from Twitter..." />
    );
  }
});
```

```
module.exports = Stream;
```

There is also no need to "require" the `snapkite-stream-client` module anymore. Next, we need to change how the `Stream` component gets its initial tweet. Let's update its `getInitialState()` method:

```
getInitialState: function () {
  return {
    tweet: TweetStore.getTweet()
  }
},
```

Code-wise, this might look like a small change, but it's a significant architectural improvement. We are now using the `getTweet()` method to get data from the `TweetStore` store. In the previous chapter, we discussed how stores expose the public methods in Flux in order to allow other parts of our application to get data from them. `getTweet()` is an example of one of these public methods, which are called *getters*.

You can get data from a store, but you can't set data on a store directly just like that. Stores have no public *setter* methods. They are purposely designed with this limitation in mind so that when you write your application with Flux, your data can only flow in one direction. This will benefit you hugely down the road, when you'll need to maintain your Flux application.

Now we know how to get our initial tweet, but how do we get all the other new tweets that will arrive later? We can create a timer and call `TweetStore.getTweet()` repeatedly; however, this is not the best solution, because it assumes that we don't know when `TweetStore` updates its tweet with a new one. However, we *do* know that.

How? Remember that, in the previous chapter, we implemented the following public method on the `TweetStore` object; that is, the `addChangeListener()` method:

```
addChangeListener: function (callback) {
  this.on('change', callback);
}
```

We implemented the `removeChangeListener()` method as well:

```
removeChangeListener: function (callback) {
  this.removeListener('change', callback);
}
```

That's right. We can ask `TweetStore` to tell us when it changes its data. For this, we need to call its `addChangeListener()` method and pass it a callback function that `TweetStore` will call for each new tweet. The question is this: in our `Stream` component, where do we call the `TweetStore.addChangeListener()` method?

Since we need to add the `change` event listener to `TweetStore` only once per component lifecycle, it makes `componentDidMount()` a perfect candidate. Add the following `componentDidMount()` method to the `Stream` component:

```
componentDidMount: function () {
  TweetStore.addChangeListener(this.onTweetChange);
},
```

We add our own `change` event listener, `this.onTweetChange`, to `TweetStore`. Now when `TweetStore` changes its data, it will trigger our `this.onTweetChange` method. We will create this method shortly.

Don't forget that we need to remove any event listeners before we unmount our React component. To do this, add the following `componentWillUnmount()` method to the `Stream` component:

```
componentWillUnmount: function () {
  TweetStore.removeChangeListener(this.onTweetChange);
},
```

Removing an event listener is very similar to adding it. We call the `TweetStore.removeChangeListener()` method and pass our `this.onTweetChange` method as an argument.

It's time to create the `onTweetChange` method in our `Stream` component:

```
onTweetChange: function () {
  this.setState({
    tweet: TweetStore.getTweet()
  });
},
```

As you can see, it updates the component's state with a new tweet stored in `TweetStore` by using the `TweetStore.getTweet()` method.

There is one final change that we need to make to our `Stream` component. Later in this chapter, you'll learn that our `StreamTweet` component doesn't need the `handleAddTweetToCollection()` callback function anymore; therefore, in this component, we're going to change the following code snippet:

```
return (
  <StreamTweet
  tweet={tweet}
  onAddTweetToCollection={this.props.onAddTweetToCollection} />
);
```

Replace it with the following code:

```
return (<StreamTweet tweet={tweet} />);
```

Now let's take a look at our newly refactored `Stream` component:

```
var React = require('react');
var StreamTweet = require('./StreamTweet.react');
var Header = require('./Header.react');
var TweetStore = require('../stores/TweetStore');

var Stream = React.createClass({

  getInitialState: function () {
    return {
      tweet: TweetStore.getTweet()
    }
  },

  componentDidMount: function () {
    TweetStore.addChangeListener(this.onTweetChange);
  },

  componentWillUnmount: function () {
    TweetStore.removeChangeListener(this.onTweetChange);
  },

  onTweetChange: function () {
    this.setState({
      tweet: TweetStore.getTweet()
```

```
    });
  },

  render: function () {
    var tweet = this.state.tweet;

    if (tweet) {
      return (
        <StreamTweet tweet={tweet} />
      );
    }

    return (
      <Header text="Waiting for public photos from Twitter..." />
    );
  }
});

module.exports = Stream;
```

Let's recap to see how our `Stream` component always has the latest tweet:

1. We set the component's initial tweet to the latest tweet that we get from `TweetStore` by using the `getTweet()` method.

2. Then, we listen to changes in `TweetStore`.

3. When `TweetStore` changes its tweet, we update the component's state to the latest tweet that we get from `TweetStore` by using the `getTweet()` method.

4. When the component is about to unmount, we stop listening to the changes in `TweetStore`.

That's how a React component interacts with a Flux store.

Before we move on to making the rest of our application Flux-strong, let's take a look at our current data flow:

*   `app.js`: This receives the new tweets and calls `TweetActionCreators` for each tweet

*   `TweetActionCreators`: This creates and dispatches a new action with a new tweet

*   `AppDispatcher`: This dispatches all the actions to all stores

*   `TweetStore`: This registers with a dispatcher and emits the change event on every new action received from a dispatcher

*   `Stream`: This listens to changes in `TweetStore`, gets a new tweet from `TweetStore`, updates the state with a new tweet, and re-renders

Can you see how we can now scale the number of React components, action creators, and stores, and still be able to maintain Snapterest? With Flux, it will always be a one-way data flow. It will be the same mental model regardless of how many new features we implement. We will benefit hugely in the long run when we need to maintain our app.

Did I mention that we're going to adapt Flux in our application even more? Next, let's do exactly that.

Creating CollectionStore

Not only does Snapterest store the latest tweet, but it also stores a collection of tweets that the user creates. Let's refactor this feature with Flux.

First, let's create a collection store. Navigate to the `~/snapterest/source/stores/` directory and create the `CollectionStore.js` file:

```
var AppDispatcher = require('../dispatcher/AppDispatcher');
var EventEmitter = require('events').EventEmitter;
var assign = require('object-assign');

var CHANGE_EVENT = 'change';

var collectionTweets = {};
var collectionName = 'new';

function addTweetToCollection(tweet) {
  collectionTweets[tweet.id] = tweet;
}

function removeTweetFromCollection(tweetId) {
  delete collectionTweets[tweetId];
}

function removeAllTweetsFromCollection() {
  collectionTweets = {};
}

function setCollectionName(name) {
  collectionName = name;
}
```

```
function emitChange() {
  CollectionStore.emit(CHANGE_EVENT);
}

var CollectionStore = assign({}, EventEmitter.prototype, {

  addChangeListener: function (callback) {
    this.on(CHANGE_EVENT, callback);
  },

  removeChangeListener: function (callback) {
    this.removeListener(CHANGE_EVENT, callback);
  },

  getCollectionTweets: function () {
    return collectionTweets;
  },

  getCollectionName: function() {
    return collectionName;
  }

});

function handleAction(action) {

  switch (action.type) {

    case 'add_tweet_to_collection':
      addTweetToCollection(action.tweet);
      emitChange();
      break;

    case 'remove_tweet_from_collection':
      removeTweetFromCollection(action.tweetId);
      emitChange();
      break;

    case 'remove_all_tweets_from_collection':
      removeAllTweetsFromCollection();
      emitChange();
      break;
```

```
      case 'set_collection_name':
        setCollectionName(action.collectionName);
        emitChange();
        break;

      default: // ... do nothing

    }
}


CollectionStore.dispatchToken = AppDispatcher.register(handleAction);

module.exports = CollectionStore;
```

The `CollectionStore` is a bigger store, but it has the same structure as `TweetStore`. First, we import the dependencies and assign a `change` event name to the `CHANGE_EVENT` variable:

```
var AppDispatcher = require('../dispatcher/AppDispatcher');
var EventEmitter = require('events').EventEmitter;
var assign = require('object-assign');

var CHANGE_EVENT = 'change';
```

Then, we define our data and the four private methods that mutate this data:

```
var collectionTweets = {};
var collectionName = 'new';

function addTweetToCollection(tweet) {
  collectionTweets[tweet.id] = tweet;
}

function removeTweetFromCollection(tweetId) {
  delete collectionTweets[tweetId];
}

function removeAllTweetsFromCollection() {
  collectionTweets = {};
}

function setCollectionName(name) {
  collectionName = name;
}
```

As you can see, we store a collection of tweets in an object that is initially empty, and we also store the collection name that is initially set to `new`. Then, we create three private functions that mutate `collectionTweets`:

- `addTweetToCollection()`, as the name suggests, adds the `tweet` object to the `collectionTweets` object
- `removeTweetFromCollection()` removes the `tweet` object from the `collectionTweets` object
- `removeAllTweetsFromCollection()` removes all the `tweet` objects from `collectionTweets` by setting it to an empty object

Next, we define one private function that mutates `collectionName` (called `setCollectionName`), which changes the existing collection name to a new one.

These functions are regarded as private because they are not accessible outside `CollectionStore`; that is, you *can't* access them like that:

```
CollectionStore.setCollectionName('impossible');
```

As we discussed earlier, this is done on purpose to enforce a one-way data flow in your application.

We create the `emitChange()` method that emits the `change` event.

Then, we create the `CollectionStore` object:

```
var CollectionStore = assign({}, EventEmitter.prototype, {

  addChangeListener: function (callback) {
    this.on(CHANGE_EVENT, callback);
  },

  removeChangeListener: function (callback) {
    this.removeListener(CHANGE_EVENT, callback);
  },

  getCollectionTweets: function () {
    return collectionTweets;
  },

  getCollectionName: function() {
    return collectionName;
  }

});
```

This is very similar to the `TweetStore` object, except for two methods:

- `getCollectionTweets()` returns a collection of tweets
- `getCollectionName()` returns the collection name

These methods are accessible outside the `CollectionStore.js` file, and should be used in React components to get data from `CollectionStore`.

Next, we create the `handleAction()` function:

```
function handleAction(action) {

  switch (action.type) {

    case 'add_tweet_to_collection':
      addTweetToCollection(action.tweet);
      emitChange();
      break;

    case 'remove_tweet_from_collection':
      removeTweetFromCollection(action.tweetId);
      emitChange();
      break;

    case 'remove_all_tweets_from_collection':
      removeAllTweetsFromCollection();
      emitChange();
      break;

    case 'set_collection_name':
      setCollectionName(action.collectionName);
      emitChange();
      break;

    default: // ... do nothing

  }
}
```

This function handles the actions that are dispatched by `AppDispatcher`, but unlike `TweetStore` in our `CollectionStore`, we can handle more than one action. In fact, we can handle the four actions that are related to the collection of tweets:

- `add_tweet_to_collection` adds a tweet to a collection
- `remove_tweet_from_collection` removes a tweet from a collection
- `remove_all_tweets_from_collection` removes all the tweets from a collection
- `set_collection_name` sets a collection name

Remember that all the stores receive all the actions, so `CollectionStore` will receive the `receive_tweet` action as well, but we simply ignore it in this store, just like `TweetStore` ignores `add_tweet_to_collection`, `remove_tweet_from_collection`, `remove_all_tweets_from_collection`, and `set_collection_name`.

Next, we register the `handleAction` callback with `AppDispatcher`, and save `dispatchToken` in the `CollectionStore` object:

```
CollectionStore.dispatchToken = AppDispatcher.register(handleAction);
```

Finally, we export `CollectionStore` as a module:

```
module.exports = CollectionStore;
```

Now that we have the collection store ready, let's create action creator functions next.

Creating CollectionActionCreators

Navigate to `~/snapterest/source/actions/` and create the `CollectionActionCreators.js` file:

```
var AppDispatcher = require('../dispatcher/AppDispatcher');

module.exports = {

  addTweetToCollection: function (tweet) {

    var action = {
      type: 'add_tweet_to_collection',
      tweet: tweet
    };
```

```
      AppDispatcher.dispatch(action);
    },

    removeTweetFromCollection: function (tweetId) {

      var action = {
        type: 'remove_tweet_from_collection',
        tweetId: tweetId
      };

      AppDispatcher.dispatch(action);
    },

    removeAllTweetsFromCollection: function () {

      var action = {
        type: 'remove_all_tweets_from_collection'
      };

      AppDispatcher.dispatch(action);
    },

    setCollectionName: function (collectionName) {

      var action = {
        type: 'set_collection_name',
        collectionName: collectionName
      };

      AppDispatcher.dispatch(action);
    }

  };
```

For each action that we handle in `CollectionStore`, we have an action creator function:

- `addTweetToCollection()` creates and dispatches the `add_tweet_to_collection` action with a new tweet
- `removeTweetFromCollection()` creates and dispatches the `remove_tweet_from_collection` action with the ID of the tweet that must be removed from the collection

- `removeAllTweetsFromCollection()` creates and dispatches the `remove_all_tweets_from_collection` action
- `setCollectionName()` creates and dispatches the `set_collection_name` action with a new collection name

Now that we've created both the `CollectionStore` and `CollectionActionCreators` modules, we can start refactoring our React components to adopt the Flux architecture.

Refactoring the Application component

Where do we start refactoring our React components? Let's start with the uppermost React component in our components hierarchy, `Application`.

At the moment, our `Application` component stores and manages the collection of tweets. Let's remove this functionality, as it's now managed by the collection store. Remove the `getInitialState()`, `addTweetToCollection()`, `removeTweetFromCollection()`, and `removeAllTweetsFromCollection()` methods from the `Application` component:

```
var React = require('react');
var Stream = require('./Stream.react');
var Collection = require('./Collection.react');

var Application = React.createClass({
  render: function () {
    return (
      <div className="container-fluid">

        <div className="row">
          <div className="col-md-4 text-center">

            <Stream onAddTweetToCollection={this.addTweetToCollection}
/>

          </div>
          <div className="col-md-8">

            <Collection
              tweets={this.state.collectionTweets}
              onRemoveTweetFromCollection={this.
removeTweetFromCollection}
```

```
                    onRemoveAllTweetsFromCollection={this.
    removeAllTweetsFromCollection} />

              </div>
            </div>

          </div>
        );
      }
    });


    module.exports = Application;
```

Now the `Application` component has only the `render()` method that renders the `Stream` and `Collection` components. Since it doesn't manage the collection of tweets any more, we also don't need to pass any properties to the `Stream` and `Collection` components as well.

Update the `Application` component's `render()` function as follows:

```
    render: function () {
      return (
        <div className="container-fluid">

          <div className="row">
            <div className="col-md-4 text-center">

              <Stream />

            </div>
            <div className="col-md-8">

              <Collection />

            </div>
          </div>

        </div>
      );
    }
```

The adoption of the Flux architecture allows the Stream component to manage the latest tweet, and the Collection component to manage the collection of tweets, whereas the Application component doesn't need to manage anything any more, so it becomes a container component that wraps the Stream and Collection components in the additional HTML markup. The Application component has become much simpler, and its markup, visually, looks much cleaner now. This improves the maintainability.

Refactoring the Collection component

Next, let's refactor our Collection component. Replace the existing Collection component with an updated one:

```
var React = require('react');
var ReactDOMServer = require('react-dom/server');
var CollectionControls = require('./CollectionControls.react');
var TweetList = require('./TweetList.react');
var Header = require('./Header.react');
var CollectionUtils = require('../utils/CollectionUtils');
var CollectionStore = require('../stores/CollectionStore');

var Collection = React.createClass({

  getInitialState: function () {
    return {
      collectionTweets: CollectionStore.getCollectionTweets()
    }
  },

  componentDidMount: function () {
    CollectionStore.addChangeListener(this.onCollectionChange);
  },

  componentWillUnmount: function () {
    CollectionStore.removeChangeListener(this.onCollectionChange);
  },

  onCollectionChange: function () {
    this.setState({
      collectionTweets: CollectionStore.getCollectionTweets()
    });
  },
```

```
  createHtmlMarkupStringOfTweetList: function () {
    var htmlString = ReactDOMServer.renderToStaticMarkup(
      <TweetList tweets={this.state.collectionTweets} />
    );

    var htmlMarkup = {
      html: htmlString
    };

    return JSON.stringify(htmlMarkup);
  },

  render: function () {
    var collectionTweets = this.state.collectionTweets;
    var numberOfTweetsInCollection = CollectionUtils.getNumberOfTweets
InCollection(collectionTweets);
    var htmlMarkup;

    if (numberOfTweetsInCollection > 0) {

      htmlMarkup = this.createHtmlMarkupStringOfTweetList();

      return (
        <div>

          <CollectionControls
            numberOfTweetsInCollection={numberOfTweetsInCollection}
            htmlMarkup={htmlMarkup} />

          <TweetList tweets={collectionTweets} />

        </div>
      );
    }

    return <Header text="Your collection is empty" />;
  }
});

module.exports = Collection;
```

What did we change here ? A few things. First, we imported two new modules:

```
var CollectionUtils = require('../utils/CollectionUtils');
var CollectionStore = require('../stores/CollectionStore');
```

We created the `CollectionUtils` module in *Chapter 8, Test Your React Application with Jest*, and in this chapter, we're using it. `CollectionStore` is where we get our data from.

Next, you should be able to spot the familiar pattern of the four methods:

- In the `getInitialState()` method, we set the collection of tweets to what is stored in `CollectionStore` at that moment. As you may recall that `CollectionStore` provides the `getCollectionTweets()` method to get the data from it.
- In the `componentDidMount()` method, we add the `change` event listener, `this.onCollectionChange`, to `CollectionStore`. Whenever the collection of tweets is updated, `CollectionStore` will call our `this.onCollectionChange` callback function to notify the `Collection` component of that change.
- In the `componentWillUnmount()` method, we remove the `change` event listener that we added to the `componentDidMount()` method.
- In the `onCollectionChange()` method, we set the component's state to whatever is stored in `CollectionStore` at that moment in time. Updating the component's state triggers re-rendering.

The `Collection` component's `render()` method is now simpler and cleaner:

```
render: function () {
  var collectionTweets = this.state.collectionTweets;
  var numberOfTweetsInCollection = CollectionUtils.getNumberOfTweetsIn
Collection(collectionTweets);
  var htmlMarkup;

  if (numberOfTweetsInCollection > 0) {

    htmlMarkup = this.createHtmlMarkupStringOfTweetList();

    return (
      <div>

        <CollectionControls
          numberOfTweetsInCollection={numberOfTweetsInCollection}
```

```
                  htmlMarkup={htmlMarkup} />

            <TweetList tweets={collectionTweets} />

        </div>
      );
    }

    return <Header text="Your collection is empty" />;
  }
```

We use the `CollectionUtils` module to get a number of tweets in the collection, and we pass fewer properties to the child components: `CollectionControls` and `TweetList`.

Refactoring the CollectionControls component

The `CollectionControls` component gets some major improvements as well. Let's take a look at the refactored version first, and then discuss what was updated and why:

```
var React = require('react');
var Header = require('./Header.react');
var Button = require('./Button.react');
var CollectionRenameForm = require('./CollectionRenameForm.react');
var CollectionExportForm = require('./CollectionExportForm.react');
var CollectionActionCreators = require('../actions/
CollectionActionCreators');
var CollectionStore = require('../stores/CollectionStore');

var CollectionControls = React.createClass({

  getInitialState: function () {
    return {
      isEditingName: false
    };
  },

  getHeaderText: function () {
    var numberOfTweetsInCollection = this.props.
numberOfTweetsInCollection;
    var text = numberOfTweetsInCollection;
```

```
      var name = CollectionStore.getCollectionName();

      if (numberOfTweetsInCollection === 1) {
        text = text + ' tweet in your';
      } else {
        text = text + ' tweets in your';
      }

      return (
        <span>
          {text} <strong>{name}</strong> collection
        </span>
      );
    },

    toggleEditCollectionName: function () {
      this.setState({
        isEditingName: !this.state.isEditingName
      });
    },

    removeAllTweetsFromCollection: function () {
      CollectionActionCreators.removeAllTweetsFromCollection();
    },

    render: function () {

      if (this.state.isEditingName) {
        return (
          <CollectionRenameForm
            onCancelCollectionNameChange={this.toggleEditCollectionName}
  />
        );
      }

      return (
        <div>
          <Header text={this.getHeaderText()} />

          <Button
            label="Rename collection"
            handleClick={this.toggleEditCollectionName} />
```

```
    <Button
      label="Empty collection"
      handleClick={this.removeAllTweetsFromCollection} />

    <CollectionExportForm htmlMarkup={this.props.htmlMarkup} />
  </div>
    );
  }
});

module.exports = CollectionControls;
```

First, we import the two additional modules:

```
var CollectionActionCreators = require('../actions/
CollectionActionCreators');
var CollectionStore = require('../stores/CollectionStore');
```

Notice that we don't manage the collection name in this component any more. Instead, we get it from our `CollectionStore`:

```
var name = CollectionStore.getCollectionName();
```

Then, we make one of the key changes. We replace the `handleChangeCollectionName()` method with a new one, `removeAllTweetsFromCollection()`:

```
removeAllTweetsFromCollection: function () {
  CollectionActionCreators.removeAllTweetsFromCollection();
}
```

The `removeAllTweetsFromCollection()` method is called when a user clicks on the `Empty Collection` button. This user action triggers the `removeAllTweetsFromCollection()` action creator function that creates and dispatches the action to stores. In turn, `CollectionStore` removes all the tweets from the collection and emits the `change` event.

Next, let's refactor our `CollectionRenameForm` component.

Refactoring the CollectionRenameForm component

CollectionRenameForm is a controlled form component. This means that its input value is stored in the component's state, and the only way to update that value is to update the component's state. It has the initial value that it should get from CollectionStore, so let's make that happen.

First, we need to import the CollectionActionCreators and CollectionStore modules:

```
var CollectionActionCreators = require('../actions/
CollectionActionCreators');
var CollectionStore = require('../stores/CollectionStore');
```

Now, we need to update the getInitialState() method as follows:

```
getInitialState: function() {
  return {
    inputValue: this.props.name
  };
},
```

Now we change it to this code snippet:

```
getInitialState: function() {
  return {
    inputValue: CollectionStore.getCollectionName()
  };
},
```

As you can see, the only difference is that now we get the initial inputValue from CollectionStore.

Next, let's update the handleFormSubmit() method by using the following code:

```
handleFormSubmit: function (event) {
  event.preventDefault();

  var collectionName = this.state.inputValue;
  this.props.onChangeCollectionName(collectionName);
},
```

We change it to this code snippet:

```
handleFormSubmit: function (event) {
  event.preventDefault();

  var collectionName = this.state.inputValue;
  CollectionActionCreators.setCollectionName(collectionName);
  this.props.onCancelCollectionNameChange();
},
```

The important difference here is that when a user submits a form, we create a new action that sets a new name in our collection store:

```
CollectionActionCreators.setCollectionName(collectionName);
```

Finally, we need to change the source of the collection name in the `handleFormCancel()` method:

```
handleFormCancel: function (event) {
  event.preventDefault();

  var collectionName = this.props.name;
  this.setInputValue(collectionName);
  this.props.onCancelCollectionNameChange();
}
```

We change it to the following code:

```
handleFormCancel: function (event) {
  event.preventDefault();

  var collectionName = CollectionStore.getCollectionName();
  this.setInputValue(collectionName);
  this.props.onCancelCollectionNameChange();
}
```

Once again, we get the collection name from a collection store:

```
var collectionName = CollectionStore.getCollectionName();
```

That's all we need to change in the `CollectionRenameForm` component. Let's refactor the `TweetList` component next.

Refactoring the TweetList component

The `TweetList` component renders a list of tweets. Each tweet is a `Tweet` component that a user can click on to remove it from a collection. Does it sound like it could make use of `CollectionActionCreators` to you?

That's right, let's add the `CollectionActionCreators` module to it:

```
var CollectionActionCreators = require('../actions/
CollectionActionCreators');
```

Then, we create the `removeTweetFromCollection()` callback function that will be called when a user clicks on a tweet image:

```
removeTweetFromCollection: function (tweet) {
  CollectionActionCreators.removeTweetFromCollection(tweet.id);
},
```

As you can see, it creates a new action through the `removeTweetFromCollection()` function by passing the tweet ID to it as an argument.

Finally, we need to make sure that `removeTweetFromCollection()` is actually called. In the `getTweetElement()` method, we check the following line:

```
var handleRemoveTweetFromCollection = this.props.
onRemoveTweetFromCollection;
```

Now, we replace it with the following code:

```
var handleRemoveTweetFromCollection = this.removeTweetFromCollection;
```

We're all done for this component. `StreamTweet` is next in our refactoring journey.

Refactoring the StreamTweet component

`StreamTweet` renders a tweet image that a user can click on to add it to a collection of tweets. You might have already guessed that we're going to create and dispatch a new action when a user clicks on that tweet image.

First, we import the `CollectionActionCreators` module to the `StreamTweet` component:

```
var CollectionActionCreators = require('../actions/
CollectionActionCreators');
```

Then, we add a new `addTweetToCollection()` method to it:

```
addTweetToCollection: function (tweet) {
  CollectionActionCreators.addTweetToCollection(tweet);
},
```

The `addTweetToCollection()` is a callback function that should be invoked when a user clicks on a tweet image. Let's take a look at this line in the `render()` method:

```
<Tweet tweet={tweet} onImageClick={this.props.onAddTweetToCollection}
/>
```

We replace it with this line of code:

```
<Tweet tweet={tweet} onImageClick={this.addTweetToCollection} />
```

The `StreamTweet` component is done.

Build and go beyond

That's all the effort that is needed to integrate the Flux architecture into a React application. If you compare your React application without Flux and with Flux, you'll quickly see how much easier it is to understand how your application works when Flux is part of it. I highly encourage you to visit the Flux official website and learn more about it at `https://facebook.github.io/flux/`.

I think it's a good time to check that everything is in perfect working order. Let's build and run Snapterest!

Navigate to `~/snapterest` and run the following command in your terminal:

`gulp`

You should see an output similar to this:

`Finished 'default' after 2.42 s`

Make sure that you're running the `Snapkite Engine` application that we installed and configured in *Chapter 1, Installing Powerful Tools for Your Project*. Now, open the `~/snapterest/build/index.html` file in your web browser. You should see the new tweets appearing on the left-hand side. Click on a tweet to add it to the collection that appears on the right-hand side.

Does it work? Check your web browser's console for any errors. No errors? Congratulations!

This is the end of our journey in learning the essentials of React.js. I am very grateful to you for investing your time and money in this book. I hope it helped you become a better React developer, and I am sure your investment will pay off very soon!

Wait, let's not stop here; let's continue with our conversation. If you have any questions left unanswered; any doubts, suggestions, ideas, or comments, or if you want to showcase your Snapterest application, then go to `https://github.com/fedosejev/react-essentials/issues` and create an issue. I'll do my best to get back to you as soon as I can.

Enjoy your React experience!

Index

Symbols

\<form\> element
  elements 108
\<input\> element
  properties 108

A

action creator
  creating 142, 143
actions 141
Application component
  refactoring 166, 167
architecture, web application
  analyzing 138, 139
arguments, componentDidUpdate method
  defining 80
arguments, componentWillUpdate method
  defining 80

B

Bootstrap framework
  URL 53
Browserify
  about 12
  URL 12
build process 12
Button component
  creating 111

C

CamelCase naming convention
  using 41
CamelCase style 82
CodePen
  about 49
  URL 49
CollectionActionCreators
  creating 164-166
Collection component
  creating 87-93
  refactoring 168-170
CollectionControls component
  creating 99-105
  refactoring 171-173
CollectionExportForm component
  creating 112, 113
CollectionRenameForm component
  creating 106-111
  refactoring 174, 175
CollectionStore
  creating 159-164
CommonJS module pattern 51
component lifecycle updating methods
  componentDidUpdate method 80
  componentWillReceiveProps method 77, 78
  componentWillUpdate method 80
  defining 76
  shouldComponentUpdate method 79
container React component
  creating 49-57

V

vinyl-source-stream dependency module
  URL 14
virtual DOM
  about 19
  defining 18, 19
  URL 19
  working 19

W

web application
  building 137
web page
  creating 14, 15

Thank you for buying
React.js Essentials

About Packt Publishing

Packt, pronounced 'packed', published its first book, *Mastering phpMyAdmin for Effective MySQL Management*, in April 2004, and subsequently continued to specialize in publishing highly focused books on specific technologies and solutions.

Our books and publications share the experiences of your fellow IT professionals in adapting and customizing today's systems, applications, and frameworks. Our solution-based books give you the knowledge and power to customize the software and technologies you're using to get the job done. Packt books are more specific and less general than the IT books you have seen in the past. Our unique business model allows us to bring you more focused information, giving you more of what you need to know, and less of what you don't.

Packt is a modern yet unique publishing company that focuses on producing quality, cutting-edge books for communities of developers, administrators, and newbies alike. For more information, please visit our website at www.packtpub.com.

About Packt Open Source

In 2010, Packt launched two new brands, Packt Open Source and Packt Enterprise, in order to continue its focus on specialization. This book is part of the Packt Open Source brand, home to books published on software built around open source licenses, and offering information to anybody from advanced developers to budding web designers. The Open Source brand also runs Packt's Open Source Royalty Scheme, by which Packt gives a royalty to each open source project about whose software a book is sold.

Writing for Packt

We welcome all inquiries from people who are interested in authoring. Book proposals should be sent to author@packtpub.com. If your book idea is still at an early stage and you would like to discuss it first before writing a formal book proposal, then please contact us; one of our commissioning editors will get in touch with you.

We're not just looking for published authors; if you have strong technical skills but no writing experience, our experienced editors can help you develop a writing career, or simply get some additional reward for your expertise.

Less Web Development Essentials
Second Edition

ISBN: 9978-1-78355-407-2   Paperback: 270 pages

Leverage the features of Less to write better, reusable, and maintainable CSS code

1. Meet the DRY (Don't Repeat Yourself) principle of software coding for your web development projects by avoiding code duplication.

2. Shorten the debugging time of complex CSS code with Less for specific devices and browsers.

3. A comprehensive, fast-paced guide that covers the essential concepts of Less through practical and well-explained code.

Mastering AngularJS for .NET Developers

ISBN: 978-1-78355-398-3   Paperback: 214 pages

Master the art of developing applications using AngularJS, ASP.NET Web API 2, and Visual Studio 2013

1. Learn how to utilize the robust features of the AngularJS framework.

2. Explore the opportunity to develop client-side applications for cross-platforms such as web and mobile.

3. Step-by-step guide with detailed instructions on how to develop and use the ASP.Net Web API with AngularJS.

Please check **www.PacktPub.com** for information on our titles

Backbone.js Patterns and Best Practices

ISBN: 978-1-78328-357-6   Paperback: 174 pages

A one-stop guide to best practices and design patterns when building applications using Backbone.js

1. Offers solutions to common Backbone.js related problems that most developers face.

2. Shows you how to use custom widgets, plugins, and mixins to make your code reusable.

3. Describes patterns and best practices for large scale JavaScript application architecture and unit testing applications with QUnit and SinonJS frameworks.

Learning Meteor Application Development [Video]

ISBN: 978-1-78439-358-8   Duration: 01:52 hours

An informative walkthrough for creating a complete, multi-tier Meteor application from the ground up

1. Master the fundamentals for delivering clean, concise Meteor applications with this friendly, informative guide.

2. Implement repeatable, effective setup and configuration processes and maximize your development efficiency on every project.

3. Utilize cutting-edge techniques and templates to reduce the complexity of your applications and create concise, reusable components.

Please check **www.PacktPub.com** for information on our titles

Printed in Great Britain
by Amazon